Life Lessons from the Game of Golf

D1489003

HONOR
B O O K S

9 8 7 6 5 4 3 2   10 09 08 07 06 05 04 03

Life Lessons from the Game of Golf
ISBN 1-56292-988-7

Copyright © 2003 Vision Quest Communications Group, Inc.

Published by Honor Books
An Imprint of Cook Communications Ministries
4050 Lee Vance View
Colorado Springs, CO 80918

Manuscript written by Steve Riach, Dallas, Texas

Contents

Foreword

There is no other game on earth quite like golf. It is a game so simple a child can play it, yet so complex, it is a source of exasperation for the best players in the world. Golf is sport's ultimate challenge. It can never be mastered. It momentarily satisfies, then leaves you staring into the face of the next challenge. This game tests you, teases you, and thrills you all at the same time. It is the definitive test of man or woman against themselves—their discipline, will, fortitude, and emotion. It is all this that makes golf, for many, the world's greatest game.

Golf tests our abilities to hit long and short, and keep it straight, to overcome obstacles. Golf is about adjusting and reacting to a variety of surroundings, elements, and situations. One hole alone does not win a round, but 18. And not just 18 together—each of them one at a time. Similarly, one shot does not win a hole, but rather a string of shots put together. The plan is to build upon small successes and finish strong, but it can not be achieved by looking at the anticipated end or the past. While it is certain that every round will generously offer a share of thick roughs, sandtraps, and out-of-bounds lies, the beauty of this game is that you can always get back on the course. Golf provides a new shot, new hole, or new day to get things straightened out and get headed in the right direction; a second chance.

This is why golf mirrors life so acutely. In golf, there is always room for improvement. Players are constantly learning, trying new things, and attempting to perfect their swings. In golf, one bad day is not a complete loss. Each round, no matter the outcome, provides at least one hole or one shot that provides a foundation for the next hole or round. On the most prominent golf courses in the world, against the beautiful backdrop of some of God's most magnificent landscapes, as well as on municipal courses in your own city or town, life's most important lessons are played out.

I have spent over 25 years in this game and have experienced wonderful thrills and difficult challenges as well. I've been blessed to win my share of tournaments in my years on the professional tour and have had the honor of prevailing in three major championships. I've witnessed historic moments and played with many of the greatest men to ever hold a club. Throughout it all, I've maintained a respect for this game and can say without hesitation that golf has taught me many significant lessons for living.

The stories of the golfers chronicled in this book are more than just experiences. They are the basis for profound Life Lessons. So, whether your handicap is 3 or 33, whether you are an avid fan or casual observer, or even if you just need inspiration, this book provides valuable insight that will do much more than help your golf score. Through the real life experiences of the men and women you will read about here, Steve Riach has provided a vehicle through which we can all view our own experience. *Life Lessons from the Game of Golf* is not just a collection of stories about the most-played sport in the world, but more than that, it is a sort of handbook for living. This book presents models of faith and principle and practical applications to help you master the most important game: life. These are Life Lessons. They are stories that will inspire you to put time-tested principles into practice in order to become one of life's true champions.

LARRY NELSON

1981 PGA Championship—Atlanta Athletic Club, Atlanta, Georgia

1983 U.S. Open—Oakmont CC, Oakmont, Pennsylvania

1987 PGA Championship—PGA National, Palm Beach Gardens, Florida

Profile of LARRY ALFORD

"Everything in life is attitude. In golf, as in life, the ones who turn the bad breaks into positive ones are the true winners."

PERSEVERANCE:

A champion finds purpose in all things.

L arry Alford was on track to becoming a member of the PGA Tour. He had a passion for golf from his childhood and felt that his future lay in the sport. But he never thought that future would have unfolded as it has.

As one of the most successful junior golfers in the United States in the 1990s, Larry won numerous tournaments in his home area of Houston, Texas. He rose to 16th on the American Junior Golf Association's national listing. In June of 1991, Larry tied with Tiger Woods for the lead of the Dinah Shore/Mission Hills Tournament as they headed into the final round. Woods pulled ahead and won. But Larry Alford demonstrated he could compete successfully under pressure. He was on his way to the next level.

But all of that changed dramatically.

That August, Larry Alford was nearly killed in an automobile accident. His injuries included a broken back, a collapsed lung, a totally destroyed facial structure, massive head trauma, and blood clots in his right arm that nearly led to amputation. The preservation of his right arm and the fact that he was still alive constituted the good news. The bad news: the injuries in his left arm necessitated amputation.

After a month in ICU, two months in brain rehabilitation, a series of grueling operations, and rehabilitation, Larry returned to the course, determined to relearn the game, using a one-of-a-kind prosthetic device customized for golf and designed by his stepfather.

"I think of it as something that can make you stronger," Alford says of his traumatic experience. "I would love to be the first pro golfer with a prosthetic hand. But I also know if I do not succeed, I won't be a failure. We only fail when we don't try, when we don't dream."

Alford's attitude inspired the golfing world. In 1992, Larry was named Junior Player of the Year by the Southern Texas PGA. That same year, PGA veteran champion Johnny Miller hosted a benefit tournament to raise funds for Larry's medical needs. A number of other Tour players have since joined in to help Larry. Their support provided the genesis for Larry's dream of playing once again.

Alford restructured his life. With that came a reevaluation of his priorities and a quick maturity. He knew golf was still a part of his future and that even in his challenging circumstances he could use golf to influence others.

Nicknamed "The One-Armed Bandit," Alford participates in golf clinics and charity tournaments all across America. He is also a highly sought after inspirational speaker. Since his recovery, he has participated in over five hundred golf and charitable events and has helped raise over five million dollars for local and national charities. He has become a living inspiration through his contagious and ever-optimistic outlook.

"Everything in life is attitude," Alford insists. "In golf, as in life, the ones who turn the bad breaks into positive ones are the true winners."

This is precisely what Larry Alford has done.

The Heart of a Champion is one that looks to turn tragedy into a triumph of spirit:

Life Lessons from the Game of Golf

Larry Alford is living proof that the circumstances of life can take away nearly everything, but they cannot take away one's heart. Larry's young world was shattered when the accident meant the end of his long-dreamed-of career. Yet Alford refused to quit on life. He refused to walk away from his passion. As a result, Alford now touches the lives of more people than if he had been able to win the U.S. Open. He is an inspiration because he never gave up.

In a famous graduation address, British Prime Minister Winston Churchill presented what is believed to be the shortest such speech in recorded history: "Never, never, never give up!" While not high-brow, Churchill's words are powerful. What better advice could a person have who is embarking on a new stage in life! It is so easy to settle for less, to let trials shipwreck our lives and keep us from moving forward. Assess yourself: Are there areas in your life where you have given up? Or do you pick yourself up and move forward toward your destiny? When mountains are in our way, we can ask God for the strength to go around them or over them; or we can watch God move them for us. But we cannot allow the mountain to make us quit.

Brothers, as an example of patience in
the face of suffering, take the prophets who
spoke in the name of the Lord. As you know,
we consider blessed those who have persevered.
You have heard of Job's perseverance and have
seen what the Lord finally brought about.
The Lord is full of compassion and mercy.

—James 5:10-11

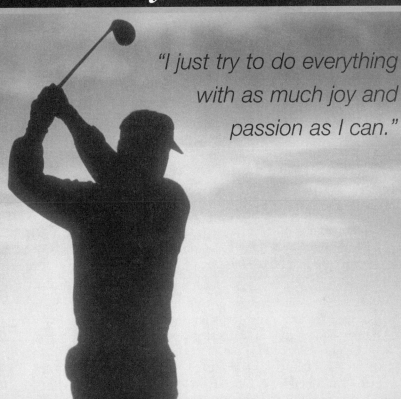

Profile of **JASON ALLRED**

"I just try to do everything with as much joy and passion as I can."

INFLUENCE:

A champion uses every opportunity to influence others.

A s the winner of the inaugural Byron Nelson Award in 2002, Jason Allred was honored as the graduating college senior golfer who displayed excellence on the golf course, in the classroom, and in the community during his collegiate career.

Allred was selected based on his senior year at Pepperdine University (2001-2002). Allred won one tournament, had two runner-up finishes and six top-ten finishes, and posted a scoring average of 72.33. He finished second at the WCC Championships and earned a place on the PING All-America third team. He was also named Academic All-American for the second consecutive year. In 1997, Allred was the U.S. Golf Association's Junior Amateur champion. He also led The Goal, Pepperdine's Christian student-athlete group.

The selection committee received several letters of recommendation and conducted interviews with each of the five finalists. Nelson himself shaped the criteria of the award: proficiency in collegiate golf competitions, success in the classroom, and character—all weighed equally.

"To think that someone has seen in me character and a passion for things I believe are important is encouraging and humbling,"

Allred said. "More than anything I'm excited and totally thankful that Mr. Nelson was directly involved."

"This award is about character and being a good person as much as it is about golf," Nelson said. "Meeting Jason told me that he was a great choice."

Allred received the award from Nelson, the award's namesake, who then invited Allred and his family to visit his ranch in Texas.

"It was a little intimidating walking up to the home of someone I'd always dreamed of meeting," said Allred. "But the second we walked in that door, we felt welcome there. That's definitely a testament to his character.

"Just listening to the stories was the best part. I could have stayed for hours to hear about everything."

Allred was humbled by being selected to receive the award named for Nelson. "To think, in some small way, they see some of those same character traits in me is definitely humbling and encouraging, too. This is probably my biggest moment in golf."

Like Nelson, Allred is a devout Christian, who wants to have a positive influence on others. "I just try to do everything with as much joy and passion as I can. I believe that's what God has in store for me," said Allred.

"If golf is what I'm going to do, I pray that golf can be my ministry. God wants us to influence the people around us. I won't be obnoxious, but I hope I can take the joy God has filled my life with and saturate the whole PGA Tour. I feel that I've been called to be a person that God can use, like Mr. Nelson, to bring light to those around them. That's what I'm passionate about. That's bigger than winning tournaments."

The Heart of a Champion is one that seizes the responsibility to influence others:

Life Lessons from the Game of Golf

Byron Nelson is a sports legend. His accomplishments on the PGA Tour will be remembered by golfers and fans for years to come. Jason Allred desires to follow Nelson. A young man, who values the positive impact he will have on people's lives over tournament victories, Allred is already making an impression.

What do people see in you when they take a good close look at who you are? Do they see your character? In ancient Greek, *charakter* means "the express image; something cut or engraved, stamped; a mark, a sign, or an impression; the exact representation of the object whose image it bore." Your character is the express image, or exact representation, of you and what has been stamped on your spirit. Thus, *your character reflects who you really are.* Whose image is stamped on you? When others inspect you, will they find the express image of Christ?

Be wise in the way you act toward outsiders; make the most of every opportunity. Let your conversation be always full of grace, seasoned with salt, so that you may know how to answer everyone.

—Colossians 4:5-6

Profile of GEORGE ARCHER

"Some day when I grow up, I'm going to play in this tournament."

VISION:

Champions pursue the vision placed in their hearts.

George Archer is one of golf's most consistent performers. He was the winner of a number of tournaments on the PGA tour in the 1960s and '70s, at a time when Jack Nicklaus and Arnold Palmer dominated the sport. In the '90s, Archer took his consistent play to the Senior Tour, where he now regularly finishes in the upper echelon of players.

But Archer will long be remembered as the winner of the 1969 Masters Championship. In '69, Archer beat Billy Casper, Tom Weiskopf, and George Knudson by one stroke to take home the green jacket.

"Winning the Masters was a great thrill," he recalls. "I won it in a very close head-to-head battle. Five fellows could have won that tournament in the last three holes. I was the fortunate enough one to be there and just keep making pars, and that was good enough to win."

Archer's first Masters memory is seemingly every bit as vivid.

"I started playing the Masters in '67; and I had a big thrill there. On Sunday, I was playing with Ben Hogan, and we were two shots off the lead. And I said to myself going out there, *You know, I don't know what's going to happen with golf today, but I'm always going to remember this round of golf I'm playing with Ben Hogan.* He [Hogan] was very nice to me that day. When we went off the first tee Ben started talking. I'm flashing through my head, *Ben Hogan doesn't talk to you; he's the quiet man.* So we walk all the way down the fairway, and he's talking away to me and finally we got to our tee shots, and I started laughing. He looked up at me, and I said, 'Excuse me, but I've got to play.' I was laughing, and what flashed through my head was, *Oh! Ben Hogan's trying to reverse psyche me.*"

But Archer says the '69 Masters title was not the biggest win in his career, not even in 1969.

"Two great things happened to me in 1969," Archer recalls. "I won the Bing Crosby and the Masters. Now, a lot of fans of the world would say, 'Well, the Masters was the thrill.' But when I was 14 years old, I caddied for Bing Crosby. And I said to myself, *Some day when I grow up, I'm going to play in this tournament.* Bing Crosby was a very nice man to young boys. He was friends with Bud Ward who was the pro at the club that I caddied at. He [Crosby] would come there during the summer maybe five or six times to play. Bud liked me, and he would see that I would get out with Crosby's bag. Because of that, the biggest thrill for me was winning the Crosby because here I got to shake Bing Crosby's hand. He kind of winked at me and said, 'Nice going, George.' He remembered me as a kid caddying for him. That was real personal with me."

The Heart of a Champion is one that focuses on the God-given vision:

Back when he caddied for Bing Crosby at his local golf club, George Archer gained a vision for one day winning the prestigious golf tournament that bore Crosby's name. From that day, Archer worked to achieve that one goal. When Archer won the tournament, he considered it a greater accomplishment than winning the

Masters. Why? Because that vision had given Archer a sense of purpose and destiny for his life.

What vision has God placed in your heart? What goals make you come alive inside? When God places a vision in our hearts, with it we receive a purpose and destiny. God's vision gives definition and direction to our lives. We have a reason to wake up each day, excited to see what God will do to further us along toward our destination. George Archer's vision gave him a purpose. What are you pursuing? How fulfilling is the process? Seek God's vision for you, and you will find purpose and destiny. Therein lies true fulfillment.

Where there is no vision, the people perish.

—Proverbs 29:18 KJV

Profiles of PAUL AZINGER

"Now I know where my happiness really comes from."

ADVERSITY:

A champion trusts even in the most challenging of circumstances.

For years, Paul Azinger played in golf's biggest events with severe pain in his right shoulder. In 1993 the source of the discomfort was diagnosed as lymphoma, a form of cancer. Azinger never complained. He merely pressed on.

Azinger first noticed shoulder pain in 1991. A biopsy was negative, but the pain never completely left. At the '93 U. S. Open, he had a bone scan of the shoulder blade and another biopsy. He refused an MRI. The pain persisted, so Azinger had another bone scan. Dr. Frank Jobe, PGA tour medical director, called Paul following the tests, telling of abnormalities showing up and again requesting an MRI. "I said, 'Look Doc, I'm playing pretty good right now. The pain usually comes at night, and I can handle it,'" Azinger remembers. "I just played through the pain.

"I never talked about it. My wife knew. My caddie knew. But it's hard to complain when you're number one on the money list and leading a major championship. It was an arc pain and didn't affect my swing."

He beat Greg Norman in a playoff at the PGA Championship that year for his first major championship. But after hurting his back before the Skins Game late in the year, Azinger finally agreed to another bone scan and MRI. This time lymphoma appeared.

"I sensed something was wrong," he said. "But you still didn't expect anybody to tell you when you're 33, you've got cancer."

With surgery, chemotherapy, and radiation, his weight dropped from 178 pounds to 158 pounds. At one point, he said, his right arm became so weak from the radiation that the only way he could lift it was with the help of his left arm. In his worst moments, Azinger leaned heavily on his wife, Toni, and his faith.

"That first chemo session was a doozy," he says. "I suffered intractable nausea and got so dehydrated that I had to be rushed back to the hospital for emergency treatment. But after a few days Toni and I flew home. Coming home is always a relief to a professional athlete, the real reward at the end of the game. This time it was even more so.

"Then one morning while I was getting ready for the day, something happened. I was standing in my bedroom praying, wondering in the back of my mind what would happen if I didn't get better. The sun was forcing its way through the blinds when suddenly a powerful feeling swelled over me like a huge, gently rolling wave lifting my feet off the sandy bottom of the seas. I stopped everything I was doing and experienced an incredible peace-giving sensation. I knew that God was with me. I felt absolutely assured that I would be okay. It wasn't that God told me what would happen next, or that the cancer would go away. I simply felt positive I was in His complete and loving care no matter what."

Today "Zinger" is both pain- and cancer-free. Yet the experience is still a constant reminder of his mortality and a lens through which he views his priorities.

"It was a life-changing experience in a lot of ways," he says. "You feel pretty bulletproof when you're 33. I look at life a lot differently now. If my doctor told me I couldn't play golf again, I'd be all right. If you have your health, you've got it all. I probably took that for granted, but I'll never take it for granted again."

The Heart of a Champion is one that trusts in God's plan even when the challenges are great:

When Paul Azinger learned that he had lymphoma, he had two choices: to feel sorry for himself and embrace the fact that cancer typically kills—or to trust that God had a plan, no matter what Paul felt or saw. He recognized that he could do nothing in his own strength to change circumstances. But he could control his outlook. So, Azinger *chose* to trust God radically. In surrendering his cancer to God, Azinger found a peace that surpassed his own understanding. No matter what, God would be with him.

Sometimes we draw a proverbial line in the sand of our faith. We can trust God for everything up to that line, but once our circumstances cross that line, we struggle to muster up that kind of trust. So, we protect our hearts from hurt, just in case God doesn't show up when we need Him. But as Paul Azinger learned, God can be trusted at all times. His promise is not that we will not experience hardship, but rather that He will be with us in those hardships and will use them to His glory and to our benefit.

Blessed is the man who fears the LORD, who finds great delight in his commands. He will have no fear of bad news; his heart is steadfast, trusting in the LORD. His heart is secure, he will have no fear.

—Psalm 112:1,7-8

RESPONSIBILITY:

Champions give out of their own experience.

O ne of the most heartwarming stories in golf history is the comeback of Paul Azinger.

Azinger was diagnosed with lymphoma back in 1993, had surgery to remove the cancer in 1994, and underwent radiation therapy for a period of time following. He made an amazing recovery and returned to golf seemingly in the same form as before his illness.

But more than his smooth and efficient form on the course, what returned even stronger was Azinger's joyful spirit. Always known as a prankster on the tour, Azinger never lost his sense of humor. He continued to bring a lighthearted atmosphere to the clubhouse. His indomitable spirit made an impression on everyone. It was as if Azinger felt it was his role to keep his peers from responding to his experience too gravely.

Once cured from cancer, Azinger also felt another responsibility—to tell others about his own personal source of strength.

Azinger has attended the PGA Tour's weekly Bible study meetings for years and has always been known as a man of deep faith. Following his ordeal, however, he seemed to have a stronger sense of responsibility to share his experience, to try to help and encourage others affected by the deadly disease.

"Obviously, I'm a much higher profile player than I ever would have been if I'd have won five major championships—because of cancer," Azinger says. "I would have to say that probably 95 percent of the people in this country have been affected by cancer at one time or another in one way or another. So I know people are really going to be interested in what I'm doing. I've had people tell me that I've been an inspiration."

This inspirational figure keeps pressing on, committed to letting his life be used to make a difference. Now, having successfully walked through his own valley of despair, he is at peace.

"I feel as secure and happy as I've ever been," says Azinger. "I'm on the backside now and, honestly, it went pretty fast. It was a wonderful time at home with my wife and kids. Now I know where my happiness really comes from."

The Heart of a Champion is one that uses personal experience for the benefit of others:

Faced with the "C" word, Paul Azinger could have folded emotionally. He could have fixed all of his attention on his health. Once well, he could have kept his emotions private. But instead, Azinger chose to use his trials and experience as a vehicle to have a positive effect on the lives of others. Clearly, Azinger understands his responsibility to strengthen others through the strength God has given him.

Paul Azinger's story is an example of how our own personal experiences can be used to affect the lives of others. So is the story of the woman at the well in John 4. After her encounter with Jesus, the woman's life was changed. So what did she do? She went back to her hometown and told everyone she knew how

Jesus changed her life. Then, their lives also changed as they encountered the Savior.

Do your experiences create graveyards for your emotions? Or do they become a source of strength and hope for others? Do you use your difficult experiences to bring others to their own encounter with Jesus?

*Many of the Samaritans from that town believed
in him because of the woman's testimony,
"He told me everything I ever did." So when
the Samaritans came to him, they urged him
to stay with them, and he stayed two days. And
because of his words many more became believers.*

—John 4:39-41

Profile of AARON BADDELEY

"To have a relationship with God, to have good family and friends, and a great wife when you get married, and that sort of thing—what else can you ask for? That's the main thing. Playing golf is just the bonus."

JOY:

A champion never loses a sense of joy.

He has been called the Australian Tiger Woods. In his native Australia, young Aaron Baddeley has equally big shoes to fill. He has been called the next Greg Norman and the greatest golf talent to come from the land down under in the current generation—true compliments for sure. Yet living up to the expectations that come with such perception can be daunting.

As a teen sensation, Baddeley won back-to-back Australian Opens in 1999 and 2000, at the ages of eighteen and nineteen respectively. The feat immediately thrust him into the golf spotlight as the next young phenom.

Baddeley responds, "Success might have come earlier than what we expected, but . . . It's been great, and I'm just enjoying it."

In the midst of the mounting hoopla, Baddeley has been steadfastly determined not to let the expectations get to him.

"I try not to. I just try and focus on what I do," Baddeley says. "I guess it is a bit annoying when I don't play as good as I want to because my expectations are higher than what anyone else can put on me."

"I've sort of improved that area a lot. . . . Just having, I guess, the inner peace is where you know things are going to turn out for the good. I just trust Him, and keep working at it."

The inner peace comes from a strong faith Baddeley first embraced when he was thirteen. His faith has kept him humble and given him a clear understanding of what is important.

Baddeley states, "You keep working at it and keep praising His name, and He does things for you and opens doors often and carries opportunities and everything—as long as you keep giving Him the glory."

"Playing golf is great; and playing for a living is awesome. But to have a relationship with God, to have good family and friends, and a great wife when you get married, and that sort of thing—what else can you ask for? That's the main thing. Playing golf is just the bonus."

"Life is so precious, and really it's so short to waste anything. So, I guess I definitely feel we need to live life to the full, and just enjoy it. And if you've got a dream, chase it."

The Heart of a Champion is one that understands God's joy was meant to be experienced:

Seeing Aaron Baddeley's combination of youth and success, observers heaped nearly unattainable expectations upon him. Yet, the blessing of Baddeley's youth has been his innocence in approaching life. He is not overwhelmed by what others predict. Rather, he has kept a very simple outlook: Life was meant to be enjoyed, not filled with burden and pressure. Because of such a perspective, Baddeley is not on the fast track to links stardom. He is simply enjoying it all.

Are you joyful about being a Christian? Well then, why don't you tell your face? How will the world be attracted to the Christian life if they never see Christians enjoying that life? Jesus was full of joy during his life on earth. How else could so many have been so irresistibly attracted to him? Are you lacking joy in your existence? If so, something is amiss. God came in the human form to give us the fullness of joy. Now happiness is not joy. Happiness is temporary. Joy lasts in spite of our circumstances. If you are missing out on the true joy of Christ, pursue it; chase after it. It is a side of God's character He wants you to experience.

> *"The thief comes only to steal and kill*
> *and destroy; I have come that they*
> *may have life, and have it to the full."*

—John 10:10

Profile of LAURIE BROWER

*"I wouldn't change
any of it, none of it. . . .
I was there for her."*

SACRIFICE:

A champion puts others first.

In 1986, Laurie Brower, then a Southern California junior golf champ and two-time Southwest Conference Player of the Year at Texas Tech, decided to try the LPGA's qualifying school. She felt ready to contend for a spot on the pro tour.

She was on her way to making it when she tore the cartilage in her wrist hitting a routine fairway shot. Her wrist became so sore she couldn't pick up a pencil. X-rays showed the bones in her wrist had fused together. Following surgery, one doctor told Brower she would never play again.

Brower spent eighteen months rehabilitating the wrist before she was ready to give the tour another shot. On the eve of making her comeback attempt, she received an urgent telephone call from her father. Laurie's mother was dying of a brain tumor.

Brower had waited a year and a half for the opportunity to prove she could play with the best golfers in the world. It was her time to shine. Yet when her dad called, she did not hesitate.

"My dad asked me to quit work. I did," Brower says. "I never asked why. It was my mother."

For two-and-a-half years in the late 1980s, Brower put golf aside and took care of her mother. On good days, her mom was normal, could hold a conversation, and remembered what life once was. Other days were far worse. "When she woke up from naps, she would scream with fear if nobody was there," Brower says. "So I tried to stay close by. I was there whenever anything bad happened."

Brower didn't care that she was losing the best years of her golf career.

"I was very thankful for that time with my mom," Brower says. "Otherwise I wouldn't have been home with her and gotten to spend so much quality time. I wouldn't change any of it, none of it. I had to watch her deteriorate; but God took her in a very gentle way, and I was there for her."

Dorothy Brower died in 1989. Shortly after, a friend asked Brower to play in a mini-tour event in Southern California. After some persuading she agreed to play.

As she stepped up to the first tee, she realized it was the same course where her mom had last watched her play. She broke down and took a nine. She doubted her ability to finish when she "realized my mom wouldn't want to see me like this," she says.

Brower rallied to shoot a 75, finished fifth, and earned $900. "It was time to get the ball rolling," she decided. Less than a year later, in October 1991, she made the LPGA Tour. It was five years later than scheduled, but Brower was much more fulfilled.

The Heart of a Champion is one that lays down personal desires for the good of others:

Laurie Brower willingly and easily laid down her lifelong dream in order to care for her mother. Why? Because she had her priorities in proper perspective. To Laurie, golf was a dream, a potential career, and a passion, but not nearly as important as her mother. Laurie sacrificed her own desires to give unconditionally of herself to her mom. Could you have done the same?

Life Lessons from the Game of Golf

People need reassurance, support, and a helping hand. They need to know they are loved. We really can't tell people *too* much that we love them. Our words are important, but our actions truly represent what is in our hearts. Jesus told us the greatest demonstration of love is to lay down our lives. Are you willing to lay down your desires for the needs of another?

"My command is this: Love each other as I have loved you. Greater love has no one than this, that he lay down his life for his friends."

—John 15:12-13

Profile of STEWART CINK

"This is golf.
This is a game.
I can handle this."

PERSPECTIVE:

Champions always remember that they are blessed.

At the 2002 U.S. Open, Stewart Cink was tied for the lead going into the tournament's seventy-second hole. Locked in a duel with eventual winner Retief Goosen at five under par, Cink's approach shot soared past the green into the rough. Goosen then landed his approach twelve feet from the pin. Needing at least a par to force a playoff, Cink then left his chip from the rough twelve feet short. His hopes for a first major title appeared over as the ensuing par putt rolled just past the cup and settled eighteen inches away. Cink was left with an eighteen-inch putt that meant nothing. Or so he thought.

"I couldn't concentrate," he later confessed. "I figured I had just bogeyed the final hole to lose the U.S. Open. I didn't think there was any way Retief would three-putt from where he was."

It was a putt Cink had made thousands of times, but the unthinkable happened. Cink pushed the next putt past the cup and tapped in for a double-bogey six to finish at three under.

Goosen watched, realizing a two-putt would clinch the Open title. But then the unthinkable happened for Goosen as well. He misfired twice, hitting his lag putt two feet past the cup, then missed that one and needed a three footer to force a playoff with Mark Brooks. He made the putt and went on to win the playoff and the Open title.

The sudden realization for Cink hit hard as he understood the lost opportunity. He told the media following the harrowing last hole, "I was feeling pretty bad for Goosen right there, because that is something that can really wreck your confidence. It really didn't dawn on me until after he had putted out and made the next one that that meant I was one shot back of the final playoff score."

Cink went home with a three-second memory of what could have been. His mother and father were teary eyed. His wife, Lisa, staggered to the players' parking lot, biting her lower lip, until she found a solitary place to sit and bury her face in her hands.

Cink, however, smiled broadly, held his two children, and shook hands with several who came by to give condolences as if they were at a funeral.

"I gave myself a darn good chance at the end, so I'm not hanging my head one bit," he said. "I'm not going to look back and say I missed a two-footer to get myself into the playoff in the U.S. Open. I'm going to look back and say I made a great effort from twelve feet to tie."

"I learned with a major championship on the line, going into the last round tied for the lead, that I can hang right in there. And that's a first time for me, being that close. So I'll take a lot out of that."

Standing before the media, Cink looked at his two young sons and remembered he had spent that very morning reading the homemade Father's Day card the boys had made him. He also remembered that the following day would be his eighth wedding anniversary. Suddenly, it hit him how blessed he was.

"I guess I should feel pretty bad, but I keep thinking of tough things that would be hard to handle. I keep thinking of Paul Azinger [overcoming cancer], and of Casey Martin [handling his leg disease]. That's stuff that would be hard to handle. This is golf. This is a game. I can handle this."

The Heart of a Champion is one that recognizes that life is full of God's blessings:

Stewart Cink's mishaps on the final hole of the U.S. Open would be an unforgettable disaster for some. But Cink realized that he is a blessed man, regardless of whether or not he wins the U.S. Open.

Disappointment and failure are very difficult to handle. But when we experience the realities of our lives in this fallen world, we gain an even deeper understanding of the full dimension of all that we have in Christ: His love, His comfort, even His sufferings here on earth to share in our struggles and human challenges. The sour in our lives does give added depth to our appreciation of the sweet. And we appreciate the value of success more when we have also experienced failure. Can we fully appreciate the blessing in our lives without experiencing disappointment?

With so much in our lives subject to the imperfect and fallen world we live in, we desperately need perspective. God has blessed us with our very breath and the beating of our hearts each day.

All you have that is good has been a gift to you from a heavenly Father who loves you beyond what you can imagine. Take a moment to reflect on the good that you have been given. Be thankful and realize that you really are quite blessed.

Don't be deceived, my dear brothers. Every good and perfect gift is from above, coming down from the Father of the heavenly lights, who does not change like shifting shadows. He chose to give us birth through the word of truth, that we might be a kind of firstfruits of all he created.

—James 1:16-18

Profiles of BOBBY CLAMPETT

"I was more concerned with my own expectations than with what other people thought about me."

SELF-CONTROL:

Champions don't let the world dictate its idea of who they really are.

An NCAA champion at Brigham Young University, Bobby Clampett had style, charisma, and a fluid swing. He was a three-time college All-American, won the World Amateur medal in 1978, and twice received the Fred Haskins Award as the nation's top collegiate player. He appeared to be headed for greatness.

"I qualified for my first U. S. Open in 1978," recalls Clampett. "I was a freshman in college."

Clampett's early exploits quickly thrust him into a role as golf's "golden boy," with stardom expected from fans and media alike.

"I guess some people tagged me as the next Jack Nicklaus," remembers Clampett. "And I think any player who has a good college career that comes out on the PGA tour with those kinds of tags put on him—that does introduce a certain amount of pressure."

The pressure was immense. Clampett hit the PGA Tour ready to fulfill the predictions as a coming champion. He won over $180,000 in each of his first two full years in 1981 and 1982, and finished those years ranked fourteenth and seventeenth. He was on his way to the top.

Profiles of Bobby Clampett

"I was 22 years old when I won my first PGA tour event, the 1982 Southern Open," he remembers. "I really thought that I would win earlier than that, but I found out when I got out there how difficult it is to win on the PGA tour, and now it's been my only win. I've had six second-place finishes. But to win the tour, a lot of things have to happen in the right way for you, and certainly winning isn't easy out there."

The realization that things might not come as easily as many predicted was reinforced during the precocious twenty-two-year-old's run for a major title at the 1982 British Open.

"I remember walking off the 72nd green at Royal Troon," says Clampett. "I had, at one point in the tournament, an 8-stroke lead and held the first-round lead, second-round lead, third-round lead. Of course my lead kept shrinking as the tournament kept moving on, and I ended up losing by 4 shots to Tom Watson. That was a difficult thing to do because certainly that was my tournament to win, but I played poorly on the weekend and didn't execute well."

Media sources began to wonder aloud whether or not their once-favored son had what it took to become a consistent winner. They questioned his heart.

Clampett remained undaunted by his critics.

"I think for me it [the pressure] was a positive because it helped me in my discipline, my preparation, and my practice routines," he says, "in that I knew that pressure was on me; and I needed to try and meet other people's expectations; but I was more concerned with my own expectations than with what other people thought about me."

Today, the situation has taken a 180-degree turn for Clampett. He is now on the other side, serving as a network television commentator.

"I have no pressure on me now," Clampett says. "Now I have this job. I'm up in the booth, and I'm talking about the game that I love. Occasionally I come out and get the clubs out of the closet, take the cobwebs off of them, and play a few tournaments. But for me now it's a lot more fun to play in tournaments because there is no pressure."

The Heart of a Champion is one that does not perform for the adulation of men:

No matter what tournament he played, reporters always referred to Clampett by connoting the dreaded "P" word alongside his name. How could Clampett be expected to live up to the potential others attributed to him? He couldn't. For Clampett, it took getting away from the pressure and pursuing another aspect of the game to gain fresh perspective and once again enjoy the sport.

The word "potential" can be a curse for us. Is it realistic to think that you can achieve the potential others attribute to you? What a comfort to know that God does not judge you based on performance. How wonderful to realize that He is not disappointed with you. The world is full of critics. Anyone can tell you what you are not. But do you really know *what you are?* God's Word states that you *are* His workmanship, to be literally translated as His "masterpiece." Not because of what you have done, but simply because of *Whose* you are.

We are God's workmanship, created in
Christ Jesus to do good works, which
God prepared in advance for us to do.
Consequently, you are no longer foreigners and
aliens, but fellow citizens with God's people
and members of God's household.

—Ephesians 2:10,19

PERSEVERANCE:

A champion never stops seeking solutions.

A ll golfers have had their share of days when nothing seems to go right. They are out of sync for a round, a week, a stretch of tournaments, even a year or more. They change caddies; they change teaching pros; they change grips; they change clubs, balls, and shoes, but none of it seems to help.

Because golf is such a mental game, some players will talk with sports psychologists or "swing doctors," practice visualization, hit for hours on the practice tees, and watch countless miles of videotape of their swing—all in the hope of recapturing something—a feel, a "zone," a sync that seems hopelessly lost.

Sometimes answers are found in the most unlikely places.

Bobby Clampett had one such experience during a tournament early in his PGA Tour career, where the answer was not found on the course.

"I think back to one unusual day I had playing with Larry Mize in the 1986 Kemper Open during the second round. I had a chronic case of the duck hooks on the driving rage. I shot a 74— not very good—in the first round. And I still had a chronic case of the duck hooks.

"I walked off the practice range rather disgusted trying to hurry to my tee time. As I was walking I saw these parallel lines in the parking lot, and I checked my stance [with the lines]. As I was doing so two gentlemen walked by and said, 'C'mon, Bobby, if you haven't found it now, you're never going to find it.'

"So I said, 'Well, I can always find it somewhere.' You never know when you're going to find it."

Fortunately for Clampett, his brief alignment check in the parking lot was just the answer he had been looking for.

"It just so happened that my stance was too close and I needed to open it up. I got on the first tee, opened my stance up, and shot a course record 64 congressional that day."

"Things can turn around very quickly in the game of golf, and that was probably one experience that really taught me a very important life lesson about never giving up."

The Heart of a Champion is one that knows God's answers can come in any form:

Bobby Clampett had searched for answers for his problems from all the typical sources. Yet in each case, he found nothing. In the quiet of a parking lot, his eyes fixed on parallel lines. In a moment the idea came, and with it a cure to his swinging ills. But had Clampett given up hope when he left the practice tees, he would not have been open to finding the answer in the parking lot. Had he listened to the spectators who suggested that there would be no answer if he had not found it on the practice tees, he would have been without hope. Yet Clampett refused to listen to the spectators and refused to give up. He knew there was an answer for him if he kept searching—even in a parking lot.

Bobby Clampett found his answer because he was open to God revealing that answer in any way God chose to do so. So often, we demand God to answer us on our terms. We want Him to show himself, or give the answer, the way we say He should. Why do we do this? Do we think we know better than the Creator of the Universe? But God does have answers to all of our problems, challenges, and questions; and those answers are perfect. He may, however, plan on answering them in a way far different than we want or expect. Our role is to stay open to His direction—at any time, at any place, in any way. We can leave the answers to Him. He is always right on time with just what we need.

Let us hold unswervingly to the hope
we profess, for he who promised is faithful.

—Hebrews 10:23

TRUST:

Champions look to heaven when they hurt.

In Bobby Clampett's golf career, he has experienced numerous challenges and struggled through a variety of adversities.

After beginning his career wearing the label of golf's next star, Clampett's career hit challenging times. In each of his first two full years on the PGA Tour, Clampett earned more than $180,000 and finished in the top seventeen on the money list. He also won the Southern Open. But those finishes would be the best of Clampett's career.

While a variety of trials ensued, clearly none was more heartbreaking than the loss of his first child in 1986.

"It was perhaps the most difficult time I've ever had in my life," says Clampett. "My wife and I gave birth to our very first child, Sarah Elizabeth, and she only lived two days. She was born with a birth defect—and we didn't know about it—called diaphramatic hernia, and she died 33 hours after she was born."

"You have to understand she was the first grandchild for both sides of the family. There was a lot of anticipation and preparation for that first child to come along, and to lose her was a very painful thing to go through."

Understandably, the experience shook Clampett to the point of causing him to scrutinize his beliefs. He came away with a stronger faith and fresh perspective.

"I came to a crossroads in my faith where I had to just trust God with that," Clampett recalls, "that He was going to work that out for a higher good. And I don't think in this life we're going to see all the higher goods that there are; I think in heaven we'll see more.

"But I've noticed a number of them while here on earth: I've watched how, unbeknownst to me, my mother lost a child that she named Sarah as well; and to watch the bond develop between my mother and my wife for the very first time that hadn't been the best of relationships to that point; the opportunities my wife and I have had to talk to people that have lost children; and the bonds that are established [as a family] when you go through it. In 2 Corinthians, Paul talks about being able to help others, give them a hope. When you go through a certain trial you can help others as well. That is something Ann and I have both been able to do and see some great things happen as a result."

For the Clampetts, seeing God work through difficult circumstances is a testament to His faithfulness.

"The Bible says in Romans 8:28 that all things work together for good to those who love God and have been called according to His purpose," says Clampett. "And certainly through my life as a believer that's been evident."

The Heart of a Champion is one that turns toward God in times of hurt:

When Bobby and his wife Ann faced the loss of their child, they had a choice—to turn toward God or turn away from Him. In their pain, they chose to turn toward Him and found comfort. They also found that God used their circumstances to give greater purpose to their lives.

Life Lessons from the Game of Golf

When we hurt, we too are faced with the choice to turn toward God or turn away. Unfortunately, many choose to turn away and believe God to be the author of their tragedy. They feel that God has somehow betrayed them or let them down. In fact, God is not the author of such circumstances, but we are, at times, subject to the consequences of a fallen and sinful world. To turn away from God will mean the hurt will be buried and never be dealt with. In turning toward Him, we will find comfort, healing, and purpose in the experience. He is the God of all comfort, who is acquainted with our sorrows. Turn toward Him in your hurt and find His comfort.

Praise be to the God and Father of our Lord Jesus Christ, the Father of compassion and the God of all comfort, who comforts us in all our troubles, so that we can comfort those in any trouble with the comfort we ourselves have received from God.

—2 Corinthians 1:3-4

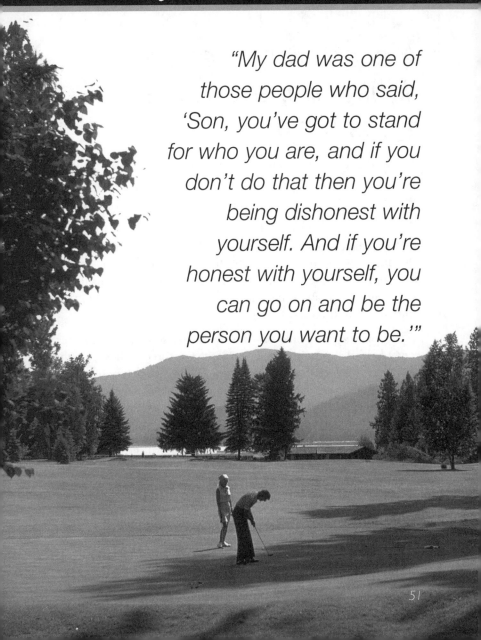

Profile of **JOEL EDWARDS**

"My dad was one of those people who said, 'Son, you've got to stand for who you are, and if you don't do that then you're being dishonest with yourself. And if you're honest with yourself, you can go on and be the person you want to be.'"

INTEGRITY:

A champion does the right thing, even when it costs him.

For twelve years, Joel Edwards had been grinding it out on the PGA tour, trying to pick up his first victory. But when Edwards stepped on the course for the 2001 Players Championship, he was feeling good about his chances in what would be his biggest tournament of the year.

On the very first hole of Thursday's first round, Edwards narrowly missed a putt for par. The ball lay but three inches from the cup. As he was getting ready to tap the ball in, just before his putter impacted the ball, Edwards noticed the ball move ever so slightly. He followed through with his stroke, and the ball rattled into the cup. It was a first-hole bogey and a start to a round of even-par seventy-two in round one. Edwards was not in bad position as he prepared for the next day and round two.

But something didn't feel right.

Edwards kept thinking about that putt. Throughout the afternoon, he replayed the image over and over in his mind and asked himself the questions: Was the ball rolling? Had he broken a rule by hitting a moving ball?

"When it first happened, I knew there was a rule or something, but I didn't lose a ball or anything like that so I just blew it off," Edwards said. "The ball turned maybe a millimeter. I said, 'I've already signed my scorecard and I'm going well. I don't think it's that big a deal.'"

But on Saturday, he decided he couldn't go on any longer without doing something. He had no idea if he had actually broken a rule, but that he couldn't get it out of his mind convinced him he needed to discuss it with an official. He went to the tournament director. Officials asked him if he had touched the ground with the putter prior to hitting the ball. Edwards said he didn't remember, but that when setting up for a shot like that he usually did touch the club to the ground, so he figured he must have done so this time. The officials said they wouldn't penalize Edwards unless he could say for certain that his club touched the ground. Unsatisfied with not knowing, Edwards disqualified himself on the spot, shook hands with the officials, and walked away with his head held high.

Edwards said, "It was not worth feeling like this."

"My dad was one of those people who said, 'Son, you've got to stand for who you are, and if you don't do that then you're being dishonest with yourself. And if you're honest with yourself, you can go on and be the person you want to be.'"

Integrity won out in the end, and Joel Edwards penalized himself even though he was unsure he had actually violated a rule.

"These rules and this sport are pure," Edwards said. "I want to know that what I earned is what I earned. This game doesn't owe anybody anything. You're blessed to be able to play it."

The Heart of a Champion is one that does what is right even when it hurts:

No one noticed what happened to Edwards' ball, and even he could not remember whether or not he had made the club touch the ground. So why would he disqualify himself? Because whether his infraction was seen didn't matter to Edwards. He would rather have walked away than think he might have won money he did not deserve. In this day of falsified financial records and corporate scandals, Edwards' actions are unusual and refreshing.

Our life is like a compass to someone who is reading us to see which way he or she should go. When we uphold our integrity, we will become people of profound influence. Are you an example of integrity for others to help show them a better way to live? True integrity is measured by how we respond in the little things that we think no one else can see. Will you set a higher standard of integrity for yourself? Or will you be disqualified?

> *"Let me be weighed on honest scales,*
> *that God may know my integrity."*

—Job 31:6 NKJV

Profile of CHARLES HOWELL III

"I've never been shy about saying I want to win the Masters. That's always been my dream. I've even joked that if I won the Masters, I'd retire the next day because that's all I want to do."

INFLUENCE:

A champion inspires dreams in others.

The seed for the improbable dream was planted in Charles Howell III in 1987. The son of an Augusta, Georgia, pediatric surgeon, Howell went with his father to the final round of the Masters Tournament. The first grader cheered wildly as fellow Augusta native Larry Mize stunned the world by nailing a 140-foot chip-in on the second playoff hole to defeat Greg Norman and win the coveted green jacket presented to the Masters champion.

Howell, who had yet to swing his first golf club, turned to his father and promptly announced his plans to win the Masters—just as Mize had done.

"It's your first Masters, you're 7 years old, and you're sitting there watching a guy from Augusta win. At that point, anything seems possible," Howell told the media corps during his first experience at the Masters as a player in 2001. "I've never been shy about saying I want to win the Masters. That's always been my dream. I've even joked that if I won the Masters, I'd retire the next day because that's all I want to do."

Howell is clearly a favored son of fans at Augusta, who hold the same hope that he will one day follow in Mize's footsteps; with or without the chip shot. Still, Howell says, the following of the hopeful throng brings no additional pressure:

"I'm not worried about the pressure or the attention," said Howell. "There's no way I'll have any more pressure than what I put on myself, because I expect a lot. I think I can win."

Howell is a long hitter with an aggressive mind-set. He goes after shots that many other players shy away from. Experts conclude his style of play is well-suited for the demanding course at Augusta National.

Of his chances for a Masters triumph, says longtime tour star Nick Price, who has known Howell since his teenage years, "I would be very surprised if he doesn't win it in his career. It's just a question of when."

Howell, is not concerned about the timing. Rather, he is simply enjoying the process. "So far, it's been a dream," he says.

The Heart of a Champion is one that follows after the example of others:

Seeing Larry Mize's incredible finish at the 1987 Masters planted an immediate dream in the heart of Charles Howell III. He saw how Mize combined a dedication to excellence to the sport with an attitude of excellence on the course and in his personal life. From that day, Howell not only wanted to win the Masters, but wanted to do so as Mize had done—not through a remarkable shot, but with the spirit of a true champion. The pursuit of that dream has put Howell well on his way to achieving his dream.

How does God put a dream in our hearts? He does so in many different ways, but more often than not, it is through the example of another. We see one who has achieved something that we too desire to bring about. When we see the essence of what we want to become or accomplish, God uses that to plant a seed in our hearts. As the seed grows, the dream is fully birthed in us and gives direction to our lives. The epitome of what we want our lives to have meant when we come to the end of our days here can now be seen in the lives of others. This is how dreams begin.

Life Lessons from the Game of Golf

Whether they seem big or small, pursue those dreams; go after them with everything within you. But do so in a manner that embodies all that is upright in the example you first saw. And remember, you too are setting an example for the next generation to follow in your footsteps.

Don't let anyone look down on you because you are young, but set an example for the believers in speech, in life, in love, in faith and in purity. Be diligent in these matters; give yourself wholly to them, so that everyone may see your progress.

—1 Timothy 4:12,15

Profile of STEVE JONES

"You are going to have troubles in your life. You won't always have mountaintop experiences. The good times never last. The bad times never last. You do the best you can and move on."

ADVERSITY:

A champion sees purpose in adversity.

In November 1991, Steve Jones crashed his dirtbike, spraining an ankle, separating a shoulder, and tearing ligaments in his left ring finger. The injured finger would keep Jones off the PGA tour for three years and force him to make a major change in his game. Most in the golf community thought he would never come back.

"At first I thought, *Well, you know, my finger's jammed a little bit, and my shoulder hurts. I'll be back in a couple of months,*" says Jones. "Next thing I know, it was two and a half years before I could even swing a club. I didn't know if I was ever going to play golf again from that injury, but I didn't feel like my career was over. It took me a year to get my swing going again."

Jones switched to a reverse overlap grip to protect his finger, which will never be completely healed. At thirty, this former up-and-coming star had to completely rebuild his game. Often, he felt like giving up. But Jones knew he still had the passion to play golf and that the talent was still there. Thousands of hours of rehabilitation finally paid off in 1996, when Jones won the U.S. Open at Bloomfield Hills, Michigan. "It was amazing to go from playing pretty well up through 1991, to all of a sudden not knowing if you're ever going to play again, to winning a major."

Tom Lehman, who is one of his best friends, might have been the only person besides Jones' wife, Bonnie, who wasn't surprised.

"People forgot how good a player he was before he got hurt," says Lehman. "When he won it [the Open] the attitude was, 'Where did this guy come from?' But Steve proved himself a long time ago," Lehman says.

And Jones never felt sorry for himself. "I always knew that God could give me my career and God could take away my career.

"Now a lot of people said, 'Why do you think this happened to you?'

"And I said, 'Well, I know why it happened; I know why I got in a motorcycle wreck.' And they said, 'You do? Why?' And I said, 'Because I was a terrible rider.'

"I knew that if God wanted me to play again, then I'd play again. I had no problem with that. I might never have won a major if I hadn't gotten injured.

"I've grown a lot through that experience. It was a great year for me, and a great year for our family to go through that. You are going to have troubles in your life. You won't always have mountaintop experiences. The good times never last. The bad times never last. You do the best you can and move on."

The Heart of a Champion is one that sees God's greater purposes when plans are sidetracked:

In the mid-1980s, Steve Jones was one of the Tour's most promising young players when the accident occurred. In the aftermath, many in the golf community were asking, "Whatever happened to Steve Jones?" In 1996, the world found out. In winning the U.S. Open the way he won it, his story drew worldwide interest. Fans around the globe were able to learn of Jones' injury, his comeback, and his faith that kept him persevering. Jones has come to the place where he is genuinely accepting of, even thankful for, the experience.

When adversity hits, do you tend to become discouraged, or do you see the bigger picture? It is very difficult to keep our joy when adversity enters our lives, but if we can understand that God uses every occurrence in our lives—good or bad—to accomplish His good purposes, we can gain new perspective. While it is inaccurate to assume God causes hardship in our lives, we *know* that He is working in every trial to bring an end result for us that is good.

We know that in all things God works
for the good of those who love him, who
have been called according to his purpose.

—Romans 8:28

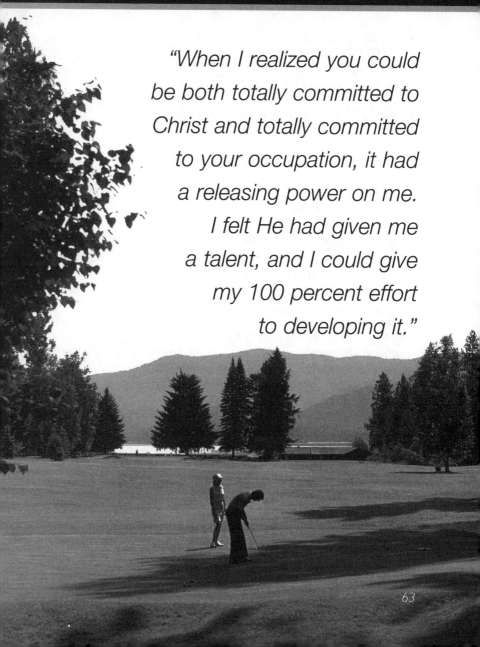

"When I realized you could be both totally committed to Christ and totally committed to your occupation, it had a releasing power on me. I felt He had given me a talent, and I could give my 100 percent effort to developing it."

DISCIPLINE:

Champions get the most out of the gifts they have been given.

Betsy King was raised in the small town of Limekiln in eastern Pennsylvania. Daily chores and duties on her family's farm forged her indomitable spirit of discipline. Competitiveness was birthed in intense games with her brother and his friends on the family basketball and tennis courts.

A knee injury in field hockey ended her run at the more physical sports, so she ended up becoming an All American in golf and led Furman University to the 1976 NCAA championship.

Turning pro in 1977, King would wait seven years to experience success at that level. But when her first win finally came at the 1984 Kemper Open, it was as if she had opened the veritable floodgates of victories. Nineteen more PGA wins came over the next five years, and King was quickly on her way to the Hall of Fame.

King credits two specific events for vaulting her into the spot as women's golf's preeminent player. "I switched teachers . . . and I became a Christian," she says. "I think I improved in all areas—emotionally, mentally, and technically."

Her association with Chicago teaching pro, Ed Oldfield, began in 1980, when Ed became King's coach and completely reworked her game over the ensuing three years.

"She had serious problems," says Oldfield. "Her divots were going way right, and the ball was going way left. I watched her play, and on one par-5 she couldn't carry a fairway wood 100 yards over water. She had to lay up with a wedge."

King arranged to spend the off-season in Phoenix—site of Oldfield's winter office. Her father accompanied her to provide support. The day of her first lesson, Betsy and her dad went out early in the morning to hit balls in private at a deserted playground.

"She was hitting balls, and I was chasing them—and a cop came and chased us," says Weir. "I think that was the low point in her career. But that afternoon Ed told me that she was going to be one of the five best players in the world."

She exceeded even the plans of her coach.

Oldfield says, "No one has ever worked harder than Betsy. She was dedicated, made lots of changes, began winning tournaments, and simply built on her success. She has no weaknesses."

"Betsy tries harder than anyone I've ever seen," says tour rival Cathy Gerring. "She's a wonderful player, and she's done great things for women's golf."

"She's one of the most focused people I've ever known, very tough and aggressive to play against," says friend and opponent Meg Mallon. "She's quiet, sure; but there's also a side to Betsy that not many people see."

The Heart of a Champion is one that puts in the necessary work to achieve the desired results:

Life Lessons from the Game of Golf

Betsy King became a champion on the LPGA Tour because of one main reason—her commitment to work hard. King is certainly a talented athlete, but without her tenacious drive to get better, King would not be in the Hall of Fame today.

Talent can carry a person only so far. In fact, the city streets are covered with gifted people who are out of work. However, what you *do* with your talent is vital. In the parable of the talents, the third man is rebuked by the master because he did nothing with what was invested in him. What talent has been invested in you by God? Work hard, study, practice, do whatever it takes to become the very best you can with the talent you've been given. That is God's design.

"To one he gave five talents of money, to another two talents, and to another one talent, each according to his ability. . . . But the man who had received the one talent went off, dug a hole in the ground and hid his master's money. After a long time the master of those servants returned and settled accounts with them. "His master replied, 'You wicked, lazy servant!'"

—Matthew 25:15,18-19,26

COMPASSION:

A champion's heart is moved by the needs of others.

Just two days after birdieing the final hole of the last tournament of the season, to lock up her third LPGA Player of the Year title in 1993, Betsy King was surrounded by Romanian street children.

In mid-November of '93, King and four fellow LPGA players had traveled with a group called Alternative Ministries to Romania for a week of work with Extended Hand of Romania, an orphan-relief group in Bucharest.

"I went from celebrating an incredible win and season to extreme sadness," says King. "I was so happy, and then it all became very, very clear. I said to myself, *How important is golf, anyway?*"

"We were standing in the snow, freezing, dealing with young children who live under a train station. It gave me a perspective that has changed my life."

King and her golfing pals stayed with a family who had no indoor plumbing. King and Alison Nicholas were so moved by the family's plight that they gave them the money to cover the cost of installing plumbing indoors.

"We experienced firsthand what it was like to live without the basic necessities that we take for granted," King says. "Their home was barely heated, but in spite of their poverty, they gave us everything they had. We ate all the time, it seemed. Their faith was so strong that it made mine even stronger."

King and her friends had gone to help, so with a renewed perspective, they visited several orphanages scattered throughout three cities, delivering food, clothing, and medicine and extending love and hugs.

"We spent a couple of days just going down to the train station and meeting kids who were living on the streets," recalls King. "We took them some food."

One night King and a local church youth group went to the train station to sing songs. Some were familiar choruses like "Amazing Grace." King was touched as she watched many of the street teens find comfort and hope through the songs and the expression of love.

In 1994, they returned to Romania to again bring needed basics to more orphaned children.

"I've never known anyone, let alone a professional athlete, who lives their faith more than Betsy," says John Dolaghan, Director of Golf Ministry for FCA. "I've never met someone with a servant attitude like hers who wants to learn more and grow. She's as authentic as they come."

Responds King: "All I can do is live one day at a time and do things with all my heart."

The Heart of a Champion is one that gives from the heart to others in need:

When Betsy King stepped on the plane in 1993 to fly from Phoenix, Arizona, to Bucharest, Romania, she did so without press coverage or fanfare. King was driven to go because of one factor:

her heart of compassion for others. Because of her actions, a handful of orphaned children today know the love of the Savior.

When a person is moved by compassion, they not only feel for those in need, but they are moved to act. The scriptures tell us that Jesus was often moved by compassion. Each time, He was touched by the needs of the people—needs that were physical [healing, feeding], emotional [suffering, instruction], and spiritual [teaching, eternal life]. In each instance, Jesus acted out of that compassion to meet the need, whether for one person or the multitude. His example shows us that true compassion is action. And when the needs of a person are met, the door is opened to meet a much greater and eternal need.

Jesus went through all the towns and villages, teaching in their synagogues, preaching the good news of the kingdom and healing every disease and sickness. When he saw the crowds, he had compassion on them, because they were harassed and helpless, like sheep without a shepherd. Then he said to his disciples, "The harvest is plentiful but the workers are few. Ask the LORD *of the harvest, therefore, to send out workers into his harvest field."*

—Matthew 9:35-38

FAITH:

A champion knows where to find all the answers.

In Betsy King's journey from fringe player to Hall of Famer, two significant events occurred in her life that put her on the right track. One was when she hooked up with teaching pro Ed Oldfield, who reworked King's swing. But just prior to her first introduction to Oldfield, King's other major realization took place: she discovered her own internal weakness.

King found herself looking for a source of inner strength and peace that was missing during those first lean years on the tour. Once again it was LPGA tour player and friend, Donna White—who had also introduced King to Oldfield—who played a key role. White was to speak at a Christian golfers' conference in 1980. King wanted to hear White speak, so she accepted an invitation to attend the conference. During one of the morning sessions, in response to a speaker's invitation, King prayed to accept Jesus Christ as her Savior and Lord. While she still had to work on the mechanics of the game, King felt for the first time that her inner game had been taken care of.

"The truth is, I don't know where I'd be if I hadn't become a Christian," says King. "But I don't think it would be where I am today. I was work-oriented, but I had a lot of my self-worth tied up in how well I played golf. I definitely feel more at peace."

That peace gave her a new fire for the game and an understanding that her fervent faith and a dedication to her game could coexist.

"I had the notion that if you were fully committed to Christ, it would mean being in the full-time ministry. When I realized you could be both totally committed to Christ and totally committed to your occupation, it had a releasing power on me. I felt He had given me a talent, and I could give my 100 percent effort to developing it.

"I saw that God wants His people in different walks of life. He can use them wherever they are—if they serve Him with all of their hearts."

"When I'm out there playing, I'm certainly going to be probably more intense than just about anybody else."

And, on most occasions, better.

The Heart of a Champion is one that understands that everything begins with God:

When Betsy King was at the bottom of her professional career, she realized that she was going nowhere with her existing approach to golf and life. So, she looked up. When she placed her life in the hands of God, she was able to place all of the weightiness of life in those same capable hands—her burdens, worries, pressure, stress—all of it. Releasing all of that allowed King to focus on developing her relationship with Christ and the talent He had given her, while letting God take care of the things which were too big for her to handle. The result has been a peace for King that has freed her to play golf with complete focus, knowing her worth is not determined by how she plays.

When Jesus told his followers in Matthew 6 to seek first the kingdom of God and His righteousness, He was telling us all what Betsy King has learned. He had just addressed a crowd concerning their needs—how they would find provision for food and clothing and other daily needs. Jesus tells the people not to be worried about those daily needs, but to trust in God, for He knows what we need and will provide for those needs. Rather, we should seek Him and His kingdom. To live in true peace means to seek God and all that is a part of His kingdom—love, joy, peace, provision. When we find that, we have found the keys to our existence. The daily details can be left in the Lord's hands.

"Seek first his kingdom and his righteousness, and all these things will be given to you as well."

—Matthew 6:33

Profiles of BERNHARD LANGER

"Number one is God, number two is family, and number three is my job. It is hard to maintain this order, and sometimes I slip; but I believe and know when you have your priorities right, everything is much easier in life."

PERSPECTIVE:

A champion knows failure is not final.

"My priorities have changed a lot since the day I accepted Christ in 1985," says Bernhard Langer. "Number one is God, number two is family, and number three is my job. It is hard to maintain this order, and sometimes I slip; but I believe and know when you have your priorities right, everything is much easier in life."

That sense of priority has helped Langer handle the challenges that come with life such as the challenge Langer faced at the 1991 Ryder Cup, perhaps the most pivotal moment of his career to that point. He was staring at the putt of his life. If it went in, the Europeans would continue a six-year dominance of the Ryder Cup. If he missed, the United States would win.

Hale Irwin, his match play foe, would later say, "There is no way I would ever, ever, ever wish what happened on that last hole on anyone. I really don't think anyone in the world could have made that putt. The pressure was unreal."

Langer's putt just missed going in. Europe had been beaten. For the first time since 1985, the Cup would stay in the United States. The final score was U. S. 14 ½, Europe 13 ½.

Delirium prevailed for the Americans. Paul Azinger rode the back of a golf cart while clutching a small American flag. Lanny Wadkins cried. And Langer played the goat.

"The first moments were hard, very hard—I can't tell you how hard," Langer admitted later. "But after sitting back and putting everything into perspective, I knew I had done my best."

Less than a week later, Langer's perspective was rewarded at the German Masters.

"This was my own tournament, as important to me as the U.S. Masters would be to Jack Nicklaus," he said. "I wanted to win that tournament so badly, but all anyone over here wanted to talk about was the missed putt. I told the press that I would talk about the putt on Wednesday, but from then on it would be a closed issue. The Bible says to forget those things which are in the past and to look forward, which is what I was trying to do."

Again it came down to a putt. This time Langer holed a fifteen-footer for birdie in a sudden-death playoff over Roger Davis to win. Later that fall he took the Million Dollar Challenge in South Africa and set a record at the time for most money ever won by an individual playing golf during one year. Langer had come all the way back.

The Heart of a Champion is one that knows God is a God of second chances:

Bernhard Langer's missed putt at the 1991 Ryder Cup was one of the most painful moments in golf. While it was a team effort, and Europe came up short as a team, still, Langer was the man on whom the loss was pinned by much of the European press. In light of that, how refreshing is Langer's perspective? "I did my best," he said in the aftermath. Because he didn't fall apart, he was ready when the next opportunity came along at the German Masters. He made that putt and won the prize because he was ready for a second chance.

Life Lessons from the Game of Golf

How do your respond to failure? Do you build on that failure and turn it into the roots for future success? Do you let that experience build your resolve and come back even more determined and eager for the next opportunity? Bernhard Langer is a great champion because he is emotionally strong and can accept the bad and good that come with the game. Langer understands that without the struggles, he cannot truly appreciate the blessings. So, with every downturn, he quickly looks for the next opportunity to succeed.

> *Brothers, I do not consider myself yet to have taken hold of it. But one thing I do: Forgetting what is behind and straining toward what is ahead, I press on toward the goal to win the prize for which God has called me heavenward in Christ Jesus.*

—Philippians 3:13-14

HOPE:

A champion knows any beginning is the start of something bigger.

Bernhard Langer is one of golf's finest international champions. The native of Germany won the Masters Championship in 1985 and in 1993 and has over 60 tournament victories worldwide. He has been a member of the European team in numerous international competitions, including the Ryder Cup and the World Cup. From 1980 to 1995, Langer accomplished a rare feat in winning at least one tournament in 16 consecutive years.

But few would have ever expected Langer to have even made it on the Tour. Raised in a poor German family, Langer was far from the privileged country club lifestyle.

"We could never afford to play golf," Langer says. "Golf was very, very exclusive and very expensive at the time. I got introduced to golf through my older brother who was caddying. He came home on the weekends or sometimes after school, went up there, and brought home a few deutsche marks. When I was eight years old, I said, 'Come on. I'm big enough. I can pull those trolleys. I can caddy. Why don't you take me along? I want to earn some money, too.'"

At first, Langer saw an easy way to earn money. Soon, however, he became hooked on the game and wanted to learn to play.

"There were anywhere from 10 to 20 caddies at the time at the local club," Langer recalls. "None of us could afford buying golf clubs. So some of the members gave us four clubs. They were obviously old. They were a three-wood, a three-iron, a seven-iron, and a putter, which had a bent shaft. They were all bamboo shafts at the time. So, we had to manage with four clubs; no pitching wedge, sand wedge, any of that. So we really had to be creative. . . . Eventually, I think when I was 14, I had saved enough money to buy my own set of golf clubs, and I was over the moon. They got polished and taken care of as if they were made out of gold and diamonds."

In 1972, a school guidance counselor asked the fourteen-year-old Langer what he was interested in as a future career. "He said, 'What are you interested in? Do you want to be an auto mechanic? Or do you want to do this or that?'" Langer recalls. "And I said, 'Well, actually I want to be a golf teacher.'

"And he says, 'What? A golf teacher? What is that?'

"I said, 'Well, someone who teaches golf. Like a tennis coach, I'd like to be a golf coach.'

"And he said, 'Well, I haven't heard of this before, so let me see if I can find anything on this profession.'"

Langer recalls the counselor leaving the room for nearly twenty minutes. When he returned, he was less than encouraging. "He came back and said, 'It's actually not an official profession in Germany.' So here I was not even 15 years old and trying to convince my parents that this is really where I see my future. This gentleman recommended for me to do something else first, to learn something 'decent before you go into that.' But I managed to convince my parents, and I went to be an assistant pro for three years. And then I joined the tour when I was 18."

The Heart of a Champion is one that sees beyond beginnings to what God is building:

From such humble beginnings, Bernhard Langer became a Masters champion and a national hero. With all that Langer did not have, he still had a dream.

The scriptures tell us not to despise the day of small beginnings. What does that mean? It means that "small beginnings" build us into something beyond what we could ever be without them. With only four golf clubs, Berhard Langer was forced to be creative in his shot making, which made him a better golfer. So, don't despise the day of small beginnings. God has a purpose in it and will use it to make you even better.

> *"Who despises the day of small things?"*
>
> —Zechariah 4:10

DILIGENCE:

A champion gleans from good examples.

Bernhard Langer is known as one of the hardest workers on the PGA Tour. After a tournament round, it is common to find Langer on the practice tees or putting greens working on his stroke until dusk. He is constantly working on every aspect of his game, trying to improve.

Langer says his work ethic comes from being raised in a poor family in war-torn Germany. His mother and father worked tirelessly to support the Langer family. His father knew the value of work, and also the value of life.

Born in Czechoslovakia, Langer's father was a Czech soldier in World War II who was captured by Russian forces.

"I think he was actually captured in France," said Langer. "They put him on a POW train heading towards Russia. When they got to the Russian border, the train stopped for a little while, and a few of them jumped out of the train and tried to escape. He [Langer's father] was one of those. They were shot at, but he escaped the bullets and the captors. He walked all the way back to Germany."

When the war was over, Langer's father settled in Bavaria, as a bricklayer.

He never forgot the price of freedom nor the merit of hard work—a lesson not lost on Langer.

"I think what I saw in both my parents was just a determination," Langer said. "Both were very determined and extremely hard workers. There was no playtime at all for them. They had to work day and night just to make ends meet and to support the three kids they had, and just to survive, actually. They built their own home all by themselves."

The lack of resources affected Bernhard and his siblings.

"Never, ever in my life did I receive any pocket money to buy something," remembers Langer. "I had to wear hand-me-downs from my older brother whether it was shoes or pants or shirts—anything."

The road from wearer of hand-me-downs to becoming a multi-million-dollar winner on the pro golf tour seems long. But Langer admits that such challenging times actually provided the groundwork for where he is today through the example of determination and effort in his mother and father.

"I think that's basically what I saw—without them teaching me a whole lot about it," says Langer. "Just watching them gave me the work ethic that I have nowadays."

The Heart of a Champion is one that sees admirable traits in others and emulates them:

The foundation for Bernhard Langer's character was built through the example of Langer's father and mother. The harrowing experience of Langer's father as a prisoner of war, and his daring escape, was an experience that Langer never forgot. To him, it demonstrated a mind set on never giving up. Langer's parents worked multiple jobs to provide sustenance for their family. Young Bernhard earned every advantage he ever received. Those experiences molded a resolute dedication to do whatever was necessary to accomplish his goals.

What traits do you look for in others to integrate into your own life? Do you admire people big on achievement, performance, or external rewards? Or do you look at the internal fabric that makes up one's true being and model yourself after those virtues? We are to remember always the things we have seen that become ways to live. Bernhard Langer saw in his parents the types of life-truths we need to engrave on our hearts. What traits are engraved on your heart from the examples in your life? Do you need to readjust your focus?

> *"Only be careful, and watch yourselves closely so that you do not forget the things your eyes have seen or let them slip from your heart as long as you live. Teach them to your children and to their children after them."*
>
> —Deuteronomy 4:9

HUMILITY:

Champions can laugh at themselves.

E very golfer has his share of humorous or embarrassing moments while going for the prize in the heat of a tournament. As everyone who has ever hit that little round ball with any club from the bag knows, once you strike the ball, anything can happen. The ball can wind up anywhere.

"There have been many times when crazy things have happened," Bernhard Langer remembers.

The first instance came in a tournament in England in the early 1980s. Langer needed three swings of the club to hit the ball twenty yards.

"I had two air shots," Langer recalls. "I was like 20 yards from the green in some heather in England. It's thick rough. I walked in there and thought, *Oh, it's going to be a terrible lie.* I go there [to the ball], and it's sitting right on top of this grass about a foot high.

"I hit right under the ball; I went under it, and the ball went down. I hit it again, and it went down. And I said to myself, *I can't believe this. You're 20 yards away and you can't hit the ball.* So, the third time I finally hit it and got it out of there. I just shook my head and said, 'You know, this is golf.'"

In Langer's second experience, he came away with a new nickname. It came in 1982 during another tournament, also in England.

"I was playing the 17ᵗʰ hole when I pulled my second shot, a nine iron, to the left. I heard the ball hit a big oak tree near the green two or three times, but never saw it come down," Langer remembers. "As I approached the green I could hear the spectators laughing. Sure enough, the ball was lodged up in the tree about 15 feet above the ground in a little indentation on a huge branch. I debated whether I should take the penalty shot or climb up in the tree and hit it. I climbed up the tree and hit it out of there."

Word of the incident had followed him across the Atlantic Ocean.

"I heard a couple in the crowd talking about me. 'There's the guy who was in the tree.' one spectator said. 'What's his name?' The other replied, 'I think it's Bernhard something.' 'No, it's not,' said the other. 'That's Tarzan!'"

"I wasn't too amused at the time. But when you look back, it's quite funny. And God puts it all in perspective."

The Heart of a Champion is one that sees lighthearted moments for what they truly are.

While all golfers often face what would be considered unplayable lies, Bernhard Langer found himself up a tree, literally. But Langer gave it his best. He simply smiled, climbed up the tree, and hit the ball. Can't you hear the crowd now calling out, "Hey, Tarzan Langer"? Langer was willing to look the fool in front of spectators because he doesn't take himself too seriously. He recognized that in some situations all you can do is laugh at yourself and make the best out of what is before you.

Everything we do in this fast-paced lifestyle is focused and intense. We rarely have a moment to laugh or to see the pure joy of a given situation. Often, God allows us to come to the end of ourselves where we can do nothing to solve a situation. The more we try, the more humorous and futile the situation becomes. We find ourselves up the proverbial tree, with our ball in an unplayable lie.

What else can we do but find the humor or joy in the situation, make the best of what is before us, and move on? Without those times, we might never fully recognize just how incapable we are of doing things without the empowerment of God. So, lighten up a bit and learn to laugh at yourself! It will do your heart good.

A cheerful heart is good medicine.

—Proverbs 17:22

Profiles of TOM LEHMAN

"I'm happy with what I've achieved. But it's more important for me, to feel like I've been used; to have meant something, to have affected other people's lives in a positive way."

SERVANTHOOD:

A champion knows that sometimes, being the best means finishing second.

During four consecutive summers—1995, 1996, 1997 and 1998—Tom Lehman either held or shared the lead of the U.S. Open after three rounds. On each occasion, he ended up making a consolation speech to the media. Those experiences left Lehman with the disappointment of being one of the world's finest golfers who never won a major tournament.

"That was always my greatest fear" Lehman says. "To die and have it written on my tombstone: 'Here Lies Tom Lehman; He Couldn't Win the Big One.'"

All of which made the finish to the 1996 U. S. Open the backdrop for interesting drama. For the final round, Lehman was paired with his friend Steve Jones. They were deadlocked after 71 holes, two pals on a stroll that would reward only one. Jones shot 69 and looked to the heavens. Lehman shot 71 and looked to next year—again.

But it is what happened en route to the final score that typifies Lehman's outlook on his 0-0 for Opens. Lehman kept Jones, playing in his first major championship since the 1991 British Open, calm. He broke the ice as they walked down the first fairway.

"We walked off the first tee, and Tom said, 'Let's pray,'" says Jones. "So Tom prayed for both of us. And put his arm around me. And we prayed walking down to the first hole. And he just basically said, 'You know, let's just glorify God today and give Him this day.'

"And I said, 'Amen. Let's do it.'"

"I could tell he was a little bit nervous," says Lehman. "Something was really in my heart—you know, here we are, two believers in Jesus Christ—maybe this could be a real example today of what it means to be Christian athletes."

Jones says, "Tom and I were walking down the 16th fairway and he shared with me Joshua 1:9, which was his verse for the year."

Lehman remembers, "I said, 'Jonesy, I want to share a verse with you,'" And I shared with him, 'Be bold and strong. Banish fear and doubt, for the Lord your God is with you wherever you go.'"

"I needed that at that point," says Jones. "Because in the U. S. Open there's a lot of pressure . . . and it really relaxed me."

"If I saw Steve Jones just walking down the street at home, I would walk over, we'd talk, and I would say something nice to him," says Lehman. "If I could encourage him in some way, I probably would. So if we are playing the last round of the U.S. Open, it shouldn't be any different. It was just so he would know that no matter what happened throughout that entire day, that God loved him."

"It was special to be with him that day," remembers Jones. "To be encouraging to me on the golf course when most guys would want to beat each other's brains out. You know, here we were good friends out on the golf course, but yet being very competitive."

Lehman's words helped inspire Jones to his amazing win in what still remains the greatest day of his professional career.

"I was disappointed in myself, but I was extremely happy for Steve," Lehman says. "I really felt like the prayer that we prayed at the beginning—that we would honor God that day—that was answered."

The Heart of a Champion is one of humility and servanthood toward others:

Placing the success of Steve Jones above his own was almost unheard of in such a high-pressure moment. But Lehman knew that in honoring God and following the scriptural mandate to "consider others above yourself," he would be doing what God wanted. He humbled himself in order to see God's greater purposes achieved.

Have you been faced with a situation in which you had the opportunity to bless another and lift them up to a higher place than yourself? Remember, Jesus Christ laid down His life so that we might receive the benefit. When we consider others above ourselves, we are very much like Jesus. This means denying our fleshly desires, putting our "wants" to death, and giving our needs to Jesus.

> *Do nothing out of selfish ambition or vain conceit, but in humility consider others better than yourselves.*
>
> —Philippians 2:3

HUMILITY:

A champion knows promotion comes from the hand of God.

Tom Lehman—Steve Jones Part II: The Rest of the Story:

F ollowing Tom Lehman's heartbreaking loss to Steve Jones in the 1996 U. S. Open, it seemed once again that Lehman had become golf's "bridesmaid."

In 1996, it was the second consecutive year Lehman had played in the final group of the U. S. Open. Both times, he watched someone else win. With similar experiences in 1997 and 1998, for Lehman, the Open was more like an open wound.

But just one month after his loss to Jones, Lehman's day arrived. He won the 1996 British Open—the major he least expected to win—en route to being the tour's leading money winner that year and being named Player of the Year. It was a highlight not only for Lehman, but also for the man he had encouraged just one month earlier.

"When he won at the British Open, it was as if I'd won it," remembers Jones.

"Steve, when I won the British Open, was one of the first people to call," recalls Lehman. "And he was so excited and genuinely excited. There's times when guys say, 'Hey, good job. I'm proud or happy for you.' And that's like the right thing to say. But his excitement was straight from the heart."

Still, Lehman has kept a clear perspective on what winning a major means.

"I think more people can relate to going through some tough times before the good times," he says. "That is where you have to keep the balance in your life. You are a golfer; that's what you do. Obviously you want to be good, but there are things beyond golf that are far more important, and that is who you are on the inside."

"I'm happy with what I've achieved. But it's more important for me, to feel like I've been used; to have meant something, to have affected other people's lives in a positive way."

The Heart of a Champion is one of humility before God:

Tom Lehman's success was in the hands of God. Similarly, King David saw God raise him up to become king of Israel after he refused to give in to ambition and to harm Saul (1 Samuel 24:1-6). As David put God's desires above his own, the Lord raised him up. Tom Lehman saw God's faithfulness in the same way. The major victory came only after he put God's desires first and blessed Steve Jones. In laying our desires down for God's, there is great blessing—even when at first it seems we are losing something precious. God always gives us back something much greater.

Have you been faced with a situation in which you had the opportunity to do the right thing, even at your own expense? How did you respond? We often don't see what God is unfolding before us. As such, what we see as good may be the precursor to something better. God promises to honor those who honor Him. He has some type of reward at the end—perhaps tangible, perhaps not. Nevertheless, the outcome is always beyond what we could have imagined.

All of you, clothe yourselves with humility toward one another, because 'God opposes the proud but gives grace to the humble.' Humble yourselves, therefore, under God's mighty hand, that he may lift you up in due time. Cast all your anxiety on him because he cares for you.

—1 Peter 5:5-7

PERSEVERANCE:

A champion refuses to quit.

n 1989, Tom Lehman had made no money to speak of as a golfer, pocketing just $80,000 over 8 years in the late '80s and early '90s. He had decided to quit and get a job. Down to the last of their savings, Lehman and his wife, Melissa, decided to take one last chance, spending their final $300 on a tournament in South Africa. That last shot became a shot in the arm, as Lehman won $30,000, setting off a new confidence and a complete turnaround of his game. Among the upper echelon of players throughout the 1990s, Lehman was named player of the year in 1996, when he won over $1.7 million. His career earnings now exceed $7 million. So it seems that $300 was a good investment.

"I wouldn't trade those years for anything," says Lehman. "I look back and there's nothing but good memories. It was difficult. You really had to want to play golf and get good in order to go through it. You have got to do whatever it takes. So I look back at that and say, 'We did it.' Melissa and I together, we did whatever we had to do to get the job done. I just wanted to get as good as I could possibly get. I didn't care if I never got rich or famous. I wanted to play because I wanted to be good. And I always believed that I had the ability to be a really good player."

No one can question Lehman's tenacity. Says Jim Flick, his teacher since 1990: "There isn't anyone who learns from disappointments as much as Tom Lehman."

To which Lehman replies, "I've had a lot more dealings with disappointment than the other extreme."

The fickle game of golf met its match in Lehman's faith. That faith carried him through the lean years and has given him perspective on his trials.

"For a while, my entire life revolved around golf," Lehman says. "When I got my priorities straight, that changed. It used to be golf first. Now it's God first, family second, golf third.

"Maybe when you deal with failure for so long, it tends to take a long time to overcome the idea you are a failure. The Hogan Tour [now Nike] was a huge step. Winning on the PGA Tour was another big step. Winning a major was the biggest step of all. So I see myself now as really being a champion. And yet, I know I am capable of being even better."

The Heart of a Champion is one that perseveres through difficult times:

Tom Lehman was down to his last three hundred dollars, yet he and his wife believed God had a purpose for Tom in the sport. Can you imagine what kind of courage that took on their behalf? It took courage to trust in God and what God had planned for their lives. He was responsible for bringing about success—as long as the Lehmans remained faithful. Tom and his wife could not have done this unless they put the failures of the past behind them and reached for the opportunity before them.

Everyone experiences failure of some sort, but past failure is really a breeding ground for future success. Don't let fear of failure disable you emotionally. Let your perseverance in the face of failure become the foundation for future success. God has great plans for your life—plans to bless you and not to harm you. He has set before you a future and a hope for your life. Trust in Him completely to bring it about.

> *"For I know the plans I have for you,"*
> *declares the LORD, "plans to prosper*
> *you and not to harm you, plans*
> *to give you hope and a future.*
> *You will seek me and find me when*
> *you seek me with all your heart."*

—Jeremiah 29:11,13

TEAMWORK:

A champion knows that together everyone achieves more.

For all his individual accolades and accomplishments, Tom Lehman insists his greatest moments in golf have come in team competition. He has represented the United States in international play as a member of Ryder Cup teams and in the President's Cup, World Cup, and Dunhill Cup competitions. It is in the Ryder Cup—the head-to-head match-ups against Europe's premier players—where Lehman has found his greatest enjoyment.

"I think maybe the highest I've ever been, the most incredible experience I've ever had on a golf course probably was the Ryder Cup in '99, and being a part of that team victory," Lehman recalls. "You know, I played team sports growing up, and there's something so special about being a part of a team. When you get a group that pulls together like that, and bonds together, and then overcomes some significant obstacles and wins—it was a great feeling. Being part of that Ryder Cup victory is definitely something I'll never forget."

But Lehman's love for teamwork extends beyond the golf course, with the "home team" being the most important.

"I'm trying not to be too cliché, but I can't think of anything more important on this earth than family," says Lehman. "I mean it's nice to play good golf; and it's nice do whatever. But when it comes right down to it, the relationships you have are the things that really give life meaning. So, it starts with family. There's nobody in this world more important than my wife and my kids."

Lehman's passion for his family and a team approach to life was birthed early on in life, through the example of his parents.

"I've learned my values from my parents, and from going to church growing up, and from friends that I have who are really committed Christian guys," says Lehman. "My dad was a professional athlete—he played football—so I learned the art of competing from him, and I think I get a lot of my work ethic and my desire from him. My mom is more the compassionate one, which is my personality. So I get a lot of that from her. My brother, Jim, is my agent; and my brother, Michael, is on the road in Scottsdale [Arizona]. So we're all still very involved with each other's lives, and that translates from generation to generation."

The Heart of a Champion is one that looks for team success above individual goals:

Tom Lehman has always been a "team player" and understands he could not have been Player of the Year or British Open champ without the many people who helped him reach the apex of his career. Even this, as Lehman readily admits, was a team effort. For Tom Lehman, life is all about "Team First."

The process of a team of people all working together to reach a goal, and then achieving that goal, is like no other experience in sport, in business, or in a family. To do this requires each member finding their own unique place in the equation and laying down personal agendas and desires to see the entire group succeed. Such is the case with God's people. As Christians, we are the body of

Christ—each with a unique and appropriate function. When we function or move together, we will find success; when we don't, we won't—it is as simple as that. Have you found your role in the body of Christ? Do you know your function? What can you do to see your "team" reach its goal in your family, occupation, school, or church? Think "Team First," rather than self first, and you will find great fulfillment and success.

Now the body is not made up of one part
but of many. But in fact God has arranged
the parts in the body, every one of them,
just as he wanted them to be. If they were all
one part, where would the body be? As it is,
there are many parts, but one body.
The eye cannot say to the hand,
"I don't need you!" And the head cannot
say to the feet, "I don't need you!"

—1 Corinthians 12:14,18-21

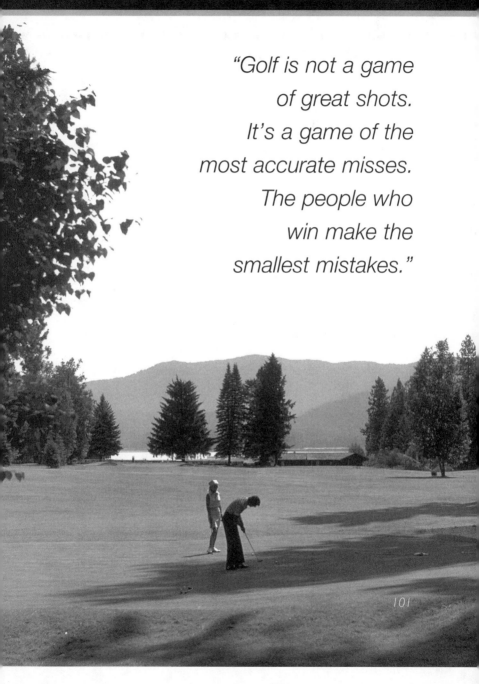

Profile of GENE LITTLER

*"Golf is not a game
of great shots.
It's a game of the
most accurate misses.
The people who
win make the
smallest mistakes."*

101

PERSEVERANCE:

A champion wins the battle of the mind.

The great Gene Littler once said of his profession, "Golf is not a game of great shots. It's a game of the most accurate misses. The people who win make the smallest mistakes."

Golf is a game made up of errors. One of the keys to succeeding is the capability of coping with failure and deficiency. Thus, mastering the art of playing golf well depends on mastering the art of playing poorly.

Many players have what it takes from the neck down to become proficient ball strikers. But it is between the ears, rather than between the greens, where even the most gifted players are defeated. Golf is indeed the cruelest of mental games.

In fact, the draw of this game is the mental challenge. Golf is a thinking-man's sport, rewarding patient players who know they must conquer all eighteen holes to be successful.

The golfer must have a plan for the entire course—knowing how to attack and what shots to hit—prior to his round. A series of right choices leads to success: what club to hit, what chance to take, when to go for it, when to play it safe, where to hit it, what type of shot to play. During play, this superfluity of information must be processed and decisions made within seconds—all without losing aggressiveness.

To excel, a player must have a keen ability to concentrate and eliminate all thoughts that conflict with his focus in order to have a true singleness of purpose. If he is emotionally distressed, he'll swing too hard, grip too tight, or rush the downswing. To control his ball, the golfer must first control himself.

Those who are champions say that when they stand over the ball, that shot is the single most important matter in their lives for that moment in time. Given the equality of talents on the tour, the one who can keep everything under control emotionally will be the winner.

The Heart of a Champion is one that keeps working to eliminate errors:

Gene Littler's comment about golf is so true. Golf has always been akin to an individual's quest for perfection. The closer one gets to being perfect on the course, the more frustrated they become as they realize they never can be flawless. Settling with imperfection is the key; to understand that not every shot will be just as you want it, but if you can lessen the distance you find yourself from the desired spot or the pin, the better off you will be. Then, the game becomes a series of strokes—each focused on individually—meant to make up a better whole.

Isn't the same true of life as well? Just as golf must be approached one shot at a time, life must be approached one day, one moment, one decision at a time. To focus on the whole thing sets us up for frustration. But to focus on one moment at a time allows us to succeed until we string together a number of successful moments.

When we see God face-to-face, we will be perfected. Until then, we will continue to make mistakes. Although we strive not to, still we will occasionally sin. Our attention must turn to eliminating as much of that sin as possible, through the power of the Spirit of God, lessening the distance between where we land and the spot of our desired goal: becoming like Christ himself. Can we do it? Yes. One "shot," or one moment, at a time.

When I want to do good, evil is right there with me. For in my inner being I delight in God's law; but I see another law at work in the members of my body, waging war against the law of my mind and making me a prisoner of the law of sin at work within my members. What a wretched man I am! Who will rescue me from this body of death? Thanks be to God—through Jesus Christ our Lord!

—Romans 7:21-25

Profiles of CASEY MARTIN

"And I've gotten to see God work in my life in a lot of ways that I would never have known had I not had the adversity."

PERSEVERANCE:

A champion sees every challenge as an opportunity.

Casey Martin is one of the world's most well-known golfers because of a major victory over disability. Martin suffers from a rare circulatory disorder called Klippel-Trenaunay-Weber Syndrome, in which blood flows down his withered right leg but it doesn't make it back up properly. Instead, the blood pools in the veins of Martin's leg, causing severe pain and discomfort. That pain increases with standing, walking, pressure, or movement—all required to play golf. Martin wears support stockings on his leg in an attempt to help push blood back up the leg. Loss of blood to Martin's shinbone has caused the bone to become weak and fragile. There is no medical solution.

"My doctor said, 'Listen, you really need to be careful if you're walking a lot,' because if I step in a chuckhole or twist my leg, I could really break my leg; it's that fragile . . . riding [in a cart] reduces some of that risk, not all of it, but some of it."

Because of his condition, Martin petitioned the PGA for the right to ride in a cart between holes of tournaments. He was denied. A series of court cases ensued, from 1997 through 2001, in a legal battle between Martin's attorneys and the PGA for the right to play.

"It got to the point where at the end of my college career, I needed to ride, and they allowed me to ride," says Martin. "When I turned professional it [the condition of his leg] continued to go downhill when I was walking. That led me to the point where I either needed to quit golf and do something else or get some help.

"A lawyer friend of mine had been encouraging me to do this, and I said, 'All right, let's do it.' I really didn't know what to expect. I didn't think it was that big of a deal. But pretty soon when I made it to the final stage of Q school it became a big deal. And then when I won that first event on the Nike tour, it *was* a big deal."

In May of 2001, in a landmark decision, the U.S. Supreme Court ruled in Martin's favor, allowing him to play PGA Tour events with the use of a cart. The decision was met by the dismay of many golf purists who felt the cart would give Martin an unfair advantage. Now Martin battles not only his disability, but also the PGA, fans, and even some of his peers who feel the sport has been compromised. Still, in the face of suffering and opposition, Martin has humbly become a symbol of courage.

"Everyone's got some struggle or hidden issue that God's allowed in their life that He can heal or He can work through. So, I'm no different than anyone else."

The Heart of a Champion is one that sees God's purpose in adversity:

At any moment, Casey Martin may find himself at a point where his condition necessitates the amputation of his leg. His efforts have not been universally supported, so he often finds himself in pairings that are less than friendly. He is frequently surrounded by fans who don't come to see him play, but rather come to see him limp. At times he feels like a sideshow participant and often feels very much alone. Yet he presses on.

What pushes us to continue in the face of suffering and criticism? What gives us endurance? It is the sense of destiny that God has put in our hearts, knowing that we have a purpose. That purpose will be fulfilled if we put the past behind us and keep pressing on. God desires for us to reach our destinies much more than we do ourselves.

> *Brothers, I do not consider myself yet to have taken hold of it. But one thing I do: Forgetting what is behind and straining toward what is ahead, I press on toward the goal to win the prize for which God has called me heavenward in Christ Jesus.*
>
> —Philippians 3:13-14

PERSPECTIVE:

A champion sees beyond the moment.

Casey Martin has persevered through the adversity of a severely debilitating disability. He has persevered in the face of criticism from fans and peers—both public and private. And he has endured becoming a figure of curiosity from the national news media. Yet through it all, he has never lost faith.

Martin, as a young man of faith, admits to having asked the typical "Why me?" questions early on. And he has always believed God could heal his condition.

"I prayed every night when I was a kid, 'Lord, heal my leg, heal my leg,' and it never happened," says Martin.

"It really wasn't until I was in college when I really got some peace about that. A friend of mine pointed out a verse from John, chapter 9, when Jesus was walking beside the road and came upon a blind man from birth. The disciples asked Jesus, 'Did this man sin? Or did his parents sin so that he would be born blind?' And Jesus told them that no, they didn't sin so that the man would be born this way, but the man was born this way so that the glory of God would be displayed. And Jesus went on to open his eyes.

"I think my eyes were opened that day to realize that I didn't do anything to deserve this [condition], but that God was going to someday do something great in my life with my leg and that He would be glorified to some extent through my birth defect. That was a few years ago, when that kind of hit home to me, and now I've seen that."

Reconciled to the realization that his physical miracle may never come, Martin has found contentment in the understanding that adversity may be a pathway to a greater purpose.

"One thing adversity does is it makes me fall to my knees," says Martin. "I pray a lot more, I seek the Lord a lot more when things are rough than when things are good. And so I'm grateful for that. And I've gotten to see God work in my life in a lot of ways that I would never have known had I not had the adversity. I guess looking at it from that perspective, it has been a blessing.

"You have to realize that adversity is going to come; but there's a loving God behind it, and He is going to do something good with it. So adversity can be a blessing in that way. And one day, when we're finally in heaven, we're going to clearly see the result of that."

The Heart of a Champion is one that sees God's greater purposes:

Casey Martin's perspective is healthy, but it has taken him years to get there. He understands that God's purpose for him may not be to work a miraculous physical healing. Martin knows that the delay in physical healing has brought about a healing of his heart. He no longer dwells on the "why?" questions. Rather, he has seen there is something great God wants to do through his circumstances to touch the world.

In many ways, Casey Martin's struggle is not unlike ours. The circumstances may differ, but the root issue is typically the same. It is so difficult for us to understand why God allows challenges to hit. Why does a loving God not answer our prayers in the way we want them answered? We must remember that we see only a part of this mysterious picture for our lives, but God sees it all. His delays are not necessarily denials. He is always working something greater in and through us, so that the character of Christ may become visible to others by being displayed in us.

As he went along, he saw a man blind from birth.
His disciples asked him, "Rabbi, who sinned,
this man or his parents, that he was born blind?"
"Neither this man nor his parents sinned,"
said Jesus, "but this happened so that the
work of God might be displayed in his life."

—John 9:1-3

Profiles of **LARRY MIZE**

"I'm only significant because God loved me enough to send Christ to die for me and for no other reason."

THANKFULNESS:

A champion savors moments in the sun.

Though he had won only one tournament during his previous five plus years on the Tour, 1987 was to be Larry Mize's year to win the big one. It was the ultimate dream come true.

"I was born and raised there in Augusta. . . . I grew up watching the pros play and worked on the scoreboards, and to play it was a dream. And then to win it was just the ultimate golfing thrill."

When all seventy-two holes of regulation had been completed, Mize was locked in a three-way tie with Greg Norman and Seve Ballesteros.

"I went out there Sunday thinking that I had a really good chance to win," Mize recalls. "I was a few shots back, nobody was paying any attention to me, and there were all the big names—Norman and Crenshaw and Seve and Bernhard Langer were up there. I was just going to try and just kind of slip in there."

Mize saw his chance almost slip away at eighteen but saved a birdie there to force the playoff. From there, it seemed the win was Mize's destiny. On the second playoff hole, it came to a dramatic end with what is perhaps the most memorable golf shot in history. With his ball resting 140 feet away from the pin, Mize calmly pulled out his sand wedge and chipped the ball into the hole to win the fabled green jacket. Few fans will ever forget the shot or the reaction from the normally laid-back Mize, who leaped into the air like he had been bounced from a trampoline.

"Once the shot went in the hole, it was just total excitement and disbelief that it went in," Mize recalls. "I think my jump and run says it all. I just couldn't believe it. I was totally elated. I just remember going crazy. I mean I started jumping up and down and running all around screaming. That's the funny thing. I was screaming. And then I realized, *You're screaming. Be quiet. . . .* but I wasn't expecting to chip it in. To chip it in to win the golf tournament was just incredible.

"The first thing I thought about after having won it was that I get to go back there every April. I get to go back home to Augusta every April for the tournament."

The Heart of a Champion is one that is full of gratitude for every blessing:

In the aftermath of his victory, Larry Mize spent time before the media, telling them of his gratefulness to God for giving him the opportunity to play and enjoy such a moment. His joy was infectious, his gratitude genuine. Mize knew the win was a gift from God. He made sure he turned the blessing back into praise and thanksgiving.

The lyrics of a popular worship chorus say, "Every blessing you pour out, I'll turn back to praise." But how often do we actually act upon those words? Every good gift comes from the Father. When the heart fails to cry out in thanks and praise to the Father for his blessings, the soul begins to imagine that those blessings are deserved, earned, or self-perpetuated. This is where we get into trouble with pride, temptation, and the desires of the flesh. Do you feel you are responsible for the blessings in your life? Or do you have an attitude of gratitude? If so, turn those blessings back to praise, and give thanks. He is worthy.

One of them, when he saw that he was healed,
came back, praising God in a loud voice.
He threw himself at Jesus' feet and thanked
him—and he was a Samaritan. Jesus asked,
"Were not all ten cleansed? Where are the other nine?
Was no one found to return and give praise to
God except this foreigner?" Then he said to him,
"Rise and go; your faith has made you well."

—Luke 17:15-19

HUMILITY:

A champion learns from mistakes.

When Larry Mize won the Masters Tournament in 1987, the feat became somewhat of a double-edged sword. The championship instantly thrust him into golf's elite.

"I think expectations went through the roof for me a little too much," said Mize. In some ways I quit being me on the golf course and started trying to be somebody else."

"I started expecting too much out of myself. It was tough on me. And for the next year or so, I didn't play that well. I would get frustrated too easily. I didn't have much patience. I was trying to play golf, but I didn't play. I tried to be longer, and just tried to change my game to get better—and I actually got worse."

Mize turned for help to Larry Moody, the Tour chaplain, who provided immediate insight.

"He really saw right to the root of the problem—that I was getting my significance from being a Masters champion," recalls Mize. "And while being a Masters champion is all well and good, you know, my significance came from my faith in Christ and not from being a Masters champion. So it was a tremendous lesson for me to learn and one I have to continue to remind myself—I'm only significant because God loved me enough to send Christ to die for me and for no other reason.

"The tough times teach us," says Mize. "I learned what's really important. Golf is important in the sense that it's what I do for a living; and it's a way of being in front of the public, how I can glorify God in what I'm doing. But, you know, the most important thing is my relationship with Jesus Christ, and keeping my eyes focused on him. After the Masters, my focus wasn't as good as it should have been. I might have lost that focus. And I learned that I have to work very hard to stay in the Bible, stay in God's Word, and keep my eyes focused on Him because that's what's important."

"Masters victories are going to come and go; they're going to end. But eternity with Christ, faith in Him, my personal relationship with Him is what will last."

The Heart of a Champion is one that remains teachable in all situations:

In sports the hardest thing to accomplish is not winning a championship, but repeating. The same is true in business or in life. Why? Because it is so easy to feel we have "arrived" when we first reach the summit of experience. We can easily become a bit prideful or find ourselves concerned with trying to live up to the expectations of those around us. When we press to achieve, we are often ineffective. Mize fell into that trap. But he took his eyes off the Masters and fixed his focus on the Master and again enjoyed playing golf.

In Matthew 14, the disciples see Jesus walking on the water toward them. Peter, never one to miss out on an experience, asks Jesus if he can come out of the boat and walk on the water. Jesus calls him to come. Peter takes the first few steps out on the water, then looks away and begins to sink. Lovingly, the Lord reaches out and catches Peter. Peter took his focus off Jesus and placed it on his circumstances, much as Larry Mize did in winning the Masters. The lessons are clear: 1) If we will simply keep our eyes focused on the Master, the circumstances will not sink us. 2) When we fall to our circumstances, He is always there to pick us up and bring us back to safety.

> *"Lord, if it's you," Peter replied,*
> *"tell me to come to you on the water."*
> *"Come," he said. Then Peter got down out of the boat,*
> *walked on the water and came toward Jesus.*
> *But when he saw the wind, he was*
> *afraid and, beginning to sink, cried out,*
> *"Lord, save me!" Immediately Jesus*
> *reached out his hand and caught him.*
>
> —Matthew 14:28-31

Profile of TERRY JO MYERS

*"It seems like a miracle
from God."*

ADVERSITY:

A champion never loses hope.

Terry Jo Myers remembers vividly the day in 1992 when she decided to commit suicide.

For nine years she had been in a constant battle with Interstitial Cystitis (IC), an incurable bladder disease. The disease caused a frequent and urgent need to urinate—as much as sixty times a day. She couldn't handle the physical and emotional upheaval one day longer.

Wracked with pelvic pain, she picked up a kitchen knife that November morning intending to cut her wrists. First, she decided to take a last look at her sleeping daughter, Taylor Jo, who was three at the time. "I looked at her, and I realized I couldn't kill myself," she says. "I couldn't leave Taylor Jo without her mother."

Terry Jo's story has a Hollywood ending thanks to a drug called Elmiron, which brought dramatic relief in 1994. Interstitial Cystitis isn't always accompanied by excruciating pain, but in Myers' case it was. "It feels like paper cuts or razor blades lining your bladder wall," Myers says. "Urine hits the 'paper cuts' and causes burning. It's intense."

In terms of life quality, IC sufferers are believed to be on par with dialysis patients at end-stage kidney failure. "It's miserable," says C. Lowell Parsons of University of California at San Diego, who pioneered the use of Elmiron. "The impressive thing with Terry Jo is she was able to function at such a high level for so long a time."

Myers suffered in silence for six years, berating herself for not having the "guts" to tell her peers. She finally went public in 1994. "It came out how painful it was, and that she considered suicide," says LPGA tour player Caroline Pierce.

She began daily doses of Elmiron as a part of a compassionate use study in July 1994. After five months, she felt much better and began to play golf without pain or symptoms for the first time since becoming ill. Now completely pain-free and symptom-free, Myers is back in the swing as a professional golfer. Just two years after finding freedom from IC, she won two events and put herself in a position to compete consistently. "It seems like a miracle from God," she says.

Myers now serves as national spokesperson for the disease, which afflicts about 450,000 Americans. She walks the halls of Congress in Washington, D.C., trying to interest politicians in bankrolling research. And she walks the fairways and greens of LPGA courses, letting fans and peers know that she has overcome.

The Heart of a Champion is one that recognizes truth even in the deepest of despair:

Terry Jo Myers nearly lost all hope. But just when she was on the verge of not being able to hold on any longer, God gave her an answer—hold on a bit longer. God did not give Terry Jo the answer she wanted. Instead, He gave her the answer she needed—that she is valuable. Once He had given her the opportunity to see that critical fact, then He gave her an answer for her physical suffering.

Life Lessons from the Game of Golf

Suffering gets our attention. Once God has our attention, He uses our circumstances to teach us deep truths that will last our entire lifetime. Are you experiencing prolonged suffering or circumstances that just don't seem to get better? When you have done everything you can to stand firm, then go ahead and stand firm. Persistence in standing will lead you to a great truth God wants you to see.

We all want God to provide answers when we want them and the way we want them, but the answers to our situation will only take care of our symptoms. God wants to deal gently with the root and give us a firm foundation for a lifetime.

Put on the full armor of God,
so that when the day of evil comes,
you may be able to stand your ground,
and after you have done everything,
to stand. Stand firm then, with the
belt of truth buckled around your waist.

—Ephesians 6:13-14

Profiles of LARRY NELSON

"Whether I was successful career-wise, tour-wise, PGA golf-wise, has really little impact on my life compared to the success I feel like that I've been as a father to my children."

PERSEVERANCE:

A champion seeks wisdom from God.

Perhaps Larry Nelson's greatest moment in golf came in 1983, at the U. S. Open at Oakmont Country Club in Pennsylvania. He shot sixty-five and sixty-seven in the final two rounds to break the USGA record for low score over the final thirty-six holes—a mark that had stood for more than eighty years.

"Winning the Open made me feel like I was both mentally and mechanically on the road [to being a consistent champion]," Nelson said. "It was a miracle that I'd made it to the PGA Tour. I had only played golf for three-and-a-half years, and the first time I tried to win my Tour card I got it. That's something that's not supposed to happen. Then 10 years later, I received the most coveted title in golf."

But over the next eighteen months Nelson would not win again. He came close a few times, but victory always seemed to elude him. Friends were asking him what was wrong. The golf media proclaimed that Nelson was in a slump. All the while Nelson couldn't figure out where he had gone awry.

"I worked on my game. I practiced. I prayed, read the Bible, met with close friends in the Tour Bible Study, but I couldn't find any answers anywhere," Nelson says. "One afternoon during the Southern Open I was practicing when it occurred to me that if God is sufficient I should call upon Him for guidance about my swing.

So I prayed right there on the practice tee and asked God to give me wisdom about what to do with my swing. I played a little better that week but didn't see an answer to my prayer."

The next week old friend Ernie Vaderson told Nelson he spotted a flaw in his swing and suggested how to correct it. Nelson tried Vaderson's recommendation, and the results were instant.

"One after another I put the ball right on the target. When I left the practice tee that day I thought to myself, *Is this God's answer?* The next day I practiced again. The control was back."

Nelson went on to win the tournament, breaking the long drought.

"When I went to the press tent, I had a chat with the Lord," Nelson said. "'Father, they're not going to believe this,' I said, 'but if they ask me how I did it, I'm going to tell them.'"

Right off the bat, a reporter asked, "Larry, how did you turn it around?" Nelson answered: "For 18 months," he said, "I've been trying everything. Last week I prayed and asked God for wisdom. He answered me."

The next day the papers carried the quote just as Nelson had spoken it.

The Heart of a Champion is one that seeks after God's wisdom:

When Larry Nelson went into a slump, he exhausted every effort to correct the problem. Nothing worked, and Nelson was out of options—except one. At the end of himself, Nelson asked God to show him what was wrong and how to fix it. Immediately, Nelson received his answer through a long-time acquaintance; and the next time he hit balls, the problem was solved. But Nelson first had to come to the end of himself and then look up.

Wisdom, the scriptures tell us, is greater than fine jewels, yet more often than not we operate in our own wisdom rather than the wisdom of God. Our wisdom is limited and will eventually fail us, but the wisdom of God is perfect and never fails. Why not seek God's wisdom first and save ourselves loads of frustration? Tapping into the wisdom of God gives us access to every answer we need.

> *If any of you lacks wisdom, he should*
> *ask God, who gives generously to*
> *all without finding fault, and it will*
> *be given to him. But when he asks,*
> *he must believe and not doubt, because*
> *he who doubts is like a wave of the sea,*
> *blown and tossed by the wind.*
>
> —James 1:5-6

FAITH:

A champion believes in a God of miracles.

As a youngster, Larry Nelson had his sights set on playing pro baseball. That dream was sidetracked when Nelson was drafted into the armed services out of high school. But today he sees how the same things that drew him to baseball eventually drew him to golf.

"I enjoyed pitching more than anything else because I felt like I could control the game," Nelson remembers. "Nobody could do anything until I threw the ball. Pitching is like golf; it's probably 90 percent mental, too—that's the same way with golf.

"I think that's the reason why I was drawn to the game."

Nelson was in his twenties and had returned from a tour of duty in Vietnam. During down times in his job with Lockheed Aircraft Corporation in Marietta, Georgia, Nelson was looking for a way to kill time and release frustration.

"I just needed something to do outside." Nelson says, "There was a driving range that was actually right across from Lockheed, and that's where I was introduced to the game. That's when I started hitting balls with a driver. It was more out of frustration probably than anything else."

What started as therapeutic recreation quickly became a passion with purpose.

"I realized that there was much more to this game than what I thought," says Nelson. "I had a chance to hang around the golf professionals. And within a very short period of time, from the spring until that fall, I had started playing really well. So I started working as an assistant pro for two years. But I never really thought I was going to do this—I never thought about being a player. I went into it much more as being a teaching professional, and then I didn't get a job that I applied for. Some of the members there (his home club) that I had become friends with said, 'Well, why don't you just try to play?' So, they put up the money and sent me to Tampa, and the next year I qualified for the tour."

"I went from watching Arnold Palmer on television to actually playing against him within four years. . . . All I knew was that I wasn't as good as the guys that I was playing against. And at each level in my golf career, I was put with a group of people that were better than I was, and I either had to learn how to compete or find something else to do. I was fortunate enough that I learned how to compete pretty well."

The Heart of a Champion is one that believes that God can accomplish the improbable:

In an era of increasing specialization in sports, it is extremely rare for an athlete to pick up a sport in his twenties and be playing professionally within four years. Nelson had enough innocence to believe God for the seemingly impossible. God brought it about and gave Nelson a platform of influence.

How far are you willing to go to trust God and know that He is bigger than any circumstance in your life? This is the same God who spoke and there was light, breathed and there was life, parted the Red Sea, made the sun stand still, sent manna from heaven, and raised the dead. He implores us to fully understand, "Is anything too hard for me?" (Jeremiah 32:27). Nothing is too difficult for God to do, no matter how hopeless your circumstances may seem. Come to the Lord with childlike faith and trust Him completely to handle the situation in His way. Come to the Father, as a small child to a parent, and behold His work.

He called a little child and had him stand among them. And he said: "I tell you the truth, unless you change and become like little children, you will never enter the kingdom of heaven. Therefore, whoever humbles himself like this child is the greatest in the kingdom of heaven."

—Matthew 18:2-4

PERSPECTIVE:

A champion knows who defines success.

One simply does not pick up a club for the first time at twenty-one years old and by the age of twenty-five begin playing against the greats of the game. Yet that's just what Larry Nelson did. Nelson broke one hundred the very first time he played a regulation course. He broke seventy within nine months and joined the Tour within four years. In 1981, just twelve years after the first day he picked up a club, Nelson won a major tournament at the PGA championship. The golf world was astonished; the experts speechless. Nelson remembers well the reaction from the press.

"Well, the first major championship I won was the PGA in Atlanta," Nelson recalls. "It really meant a lot to me because after you win a few tournaments then everybody says, 'Well, you know, he's not really a great player or one of the top players until he wins one of the Majors.'. . . So, I won the PGA.

"So the next thing was, 'Well, you're not really a great player until you win two Majors.' So then I won the U. S. Open in 1983 and a couple of tournaments in between.

"Then they say, 'Well, yeah, a lot of people have won two Majors.' And then when I won the third [major], for me there was a lot of self-satisfaction. But from the outside golfing world and the news media, it was kind of looked on as a fluke simply because I did not have any amateur background playing in college. This was something that wasn't supposed to happen. So it was pretty much dismissed by a lot of people. But I got a lot of great satisfaction out of that."

Nelson's wins at the U.S. Open in 1983 and the PGA Championship in 1981 and 1987 showed just what a talented player he had become. He stared down defending champ Tom Watson at the Open and beat him by one stroke in the last round. At the PGA, he ran away from Fuzzy Zoeller in '81 and out-dueled Lanny Wadkins in a playoff in '87. During the decade of the '80s, Nelson joined Watson, Jack Nicklaus, and Seve Ballesteros as the only four players to win three or more majors. Yet few in the golf circles even took notice.

"I mean if you asked a trivia question of the four people who won at least three Majors in the 1980s, they could probably come up with three of the four names; and mine would be the fourth.

"This is kind of a game sometimes that you have to be satisfied with your achievements. Somebody explained to me that success is being happy with what you had. So I feel like I'm very successful."

The Heart of a Champion is one that understands the standards of God and men are different:

Larry Nelson has never received proper credit for the outstanding golfer he has become, even with three victories in majors. But Nelson has maintained perspective, knowing that he found personal satisfaction in what he accomplished, and that his identity comes from a source other than the public or press.

It was legendary basketball coach John Wooden who said, "Success is peace of mind which is a direct result of self-satisfaction in knowing you did your best to become the best that you are capable of becoming." This describes the attitude we should have of our own lives. We can never measure our own success based on judgments of the surrounding world. We will never be satisfied; we'll be hungering for more to feed our pride or to soothe our wounds. A man or woman of God learns to be content to be the person God has fashioned them to be and to give the very best they can give in all situations. In light of that, are you successful?

We are not trying to please men
but God, who tests our hearts.
We were not looking for praise from men.

—1 Thessalonians 2:4,6

LEADERSHIP:

A champion thinks family first.

E ven in winning three major tournaments, Larry Nelson never seemed to allow his priorities to become skewed. It was evident to his peers that Nelson was not in the game to succeed at any cost. In fact, golf often took a backseat to more important things, and the temporal aspect of the victories helped shape his sense of success.

"I don't think being on the tour really gave me that sense of success," Nelson said. "I think it was more from a biblical basis, and the really good advice from some good Christian friends that I had. All the teachings that I had really kind of helped define what success is.

"There's always a tag line to my name, which is nice. I mean it's nice when they introduce you as a three-time Major championship winner. I think from us being human, we enjoy that type of thing; we enjoy being recognized and our accomplishments being recognized, because people want to be successful in what they do. And I've been fortunate in that regard in that I've had a lot of accomplishments. But if my focus had been on what I didn't do from reading the papers and some of the magazine articles and stuff, then I would be a very disappointed man. Success is not really derived from what I do, but Who I know. Without that, I wouldn't be as happy as I am right now."

For Nelson, happiness has come from the peace of mind he has gained from making decisions based on conviction rather than apparent necessity. That has meant often laying golf down when other needs took precedence.

"During the middle part of my career, in my early to mid-thirties, I spent 15 weeks on the tour, and the rest of the time I spent at home with my family," Nelson remembers, "simply because my kids were growing up. They needed soccer coaches. They needed little league coaches, and basketball coaches; and I really wanted to be in their life.

"Someone told me early on, right when Drew, my first child was born, 'I've never heard a successful businessman say, Gee, I wish I had spent more time at work. It was always, I wish I had spent more time with my family.'"

When Nelson himself counted the cost, the choice to put golf second was an easy one.

"I didn't want to get to over 50 years old like I am right now, and look back and say, 'Gee, I wish I had spent more time with my kids,'" he says. "Whether I was successful career-wise, tour-wise, PGA golf-wise, has really little impact on my life compared to the success I feel like that I've been as a father to my children."

The Heart of a Champion is one that understands what is most important:

Larry Nelson was never willing to sacrifice the emotional health of his family for the lure of fame and material success. He knew that no number of championships, trophies, or large paydays could ever take the place of key moments in the lives of his wife and children. So, at times, he set aside his career to be involved with his family. Because of that choice, Nelson has lived a family life without regret.

In this age, we are tugged in all directions, attempting to climb the ladder of success, to become someone of importance, to stake our claim in life and be identified with something we have accomplished. Yet, in the midst of this race, many have abandoned their primary role with their families. There is no greater legacy we can leave on this earth than generations to follow in our lineage that are filled with individuals and families demonstrating the character of Christ. So, what is the priority in your life—worldly "success" or your family?

Husbands, love your wives, just as Christ loved the church and gave himself up for her. Fathers, do not exasperate your children; instead, bring them up in the training and instruction of the Lord.

—Ephesians 5:25, 6:4

Profile of JACK NICKLAUS

"She's [Barbara, his wife] really made her life second to mine. She's never said, 'Jack we're going to do this.' She'll always say, 'We've got your schedule. We'll do this. Then if we have time, we'll do the other.'"

SACRIFICE:

A champion puts the needs of family first.

J ack Nicklaus is considered by many to be the greatest golfer ever. When he came onto the scene in the early 1960s, Nicklaus revolutionized the game. He hit the ball farther than anyone else and demonstrated the precision of a surgeon, the nerves of a cat burglar, and the heart of a lion. The man known as "The Golden Bear" dominated the sport and established a new standard while leaving the other players in his wake.

Nicklaus' record shows a total of seventy tournament wins—second all-time, with victories in an unprecedented twenty major championships. He finished in the top five of fifty-six Grand Slam championships and won each of those titles at least three times, including six Masters titles.

What the record does not show is the person Nicklaus says is most responsible for his success. It is not his coach, agent, or teaching pro. Rather, it is, according to Nicklaus, his wife Barbara.

For forty years, the wife of golfing legend Jack Nicklaus, or "Momma Bear" as she is affectionately known, has been the strength behind the Nicklaus family, which includes five grown children. For those interested in seeing an example of a professional athlete's wife who is a model of faith, many who know her would point to Barbara Nicklaus.

Of Jack's eighteen major championships, he figures Barbara "has meant at least fifteen" to him. This is due, the golfing legend says, partly to her undying support, and also because she has been "99 percent responsible" for raising their kids.

Barbara says her faith in Christ and her prayer life have been her source of strength during a challenging lifestyle. As such, she has been a true picture of humility and self-sacrifice, an example that has not gone unnoticed.

"She's really made her life second to mine," Jack told the Palm Beach Post. "She's never said, 'Jack we're going to do this.' She'll always say, 'We've got your schedule. We'll do this. Then if we have time, we'll do the other.'"

For her lifetime of support and example, Barbara was given the inaugural PGA First Lady of Golf Award in 1999.

More than that, she has received the constant praise of her husband and peace in knowing she has followed God's plan for her life.

The Heart of a Champion is one that sacrifices personal goals for the benefit of others:

Jack Nicklaus is an American institution. When he joined the PGA Tour, he quickly became the greatest player ever to hit the links. But as with most superstars in sports, entertainment, business, or politics, he could not have succeeded to the extent he did without someone standing firmly behind and beside him. Barbara Nicklaus' sacrifice to lay down her life so that her husband could become a champion has allowed him to touch the lives of literally millions of people around the world, and allowed those millions of fans to behold the exploits of one of the greatest sports performers ever.

Life Lessons from the Game of Golf

What are you willing to lay down in order that another may succeed? The nature of God is selflessness. Jesus laid down his life so that we might be elevated and find redemption and salvation. The joy set before Jesus was His making a way for our destiny to be fulfilled. In the spirit of Christ, we are exhorted to do the same. In laying down our desires and supporting others as they reach their goals, we become like Christ. Humble yourself to lift others up so they can see their destinies fulfilled. The joy you will receive in return will be beyond what you would receive from seeing your own goals fulfilled.

Let us fix our eyes on Jesus, the author and perfector of our faith, who for the joy set before him endured the cross, scorning its shame, and sat down at the right hand of the throne of God.

—Hebrews 12:2

Profiles of GARY PLAYER

"Your faith has got to be the most important thing because that's where you get all your guidance from and all your strength."

INFLUENCE:

Champions understand responsibility.

G ary Player is one of the most celebrated golfers in the world. The native of South Africa is the only player in the twentieth century to win the British Open in three decades—winning the title in 1959, 1968, and 1974.

In 2001, Player participated in his final British Open. As he walked to the eighteenth green one last time, he was greeted by thousands of fans rising to their feet to cheer the man who had given them so many great moments.

But Player has given great memories to many around the golf world. He won twenty-one tournaments on the PGA Tour, including victories in each of the four majors. Along with his triumphs at the British, he won the PGA Championship in 1962 and 1972; the U.S. Open in 1965; and the Masters in 1961 and 1974—becoming just the third golfer ever to win the coveted "grand slam." He is truly a golf legend, who has remained active on the Senior Tour into his sixties.

"When you play other sports you almost finish at the age of 30. Now, isn't it nice that you can play golf and be playing very well at the age of 70?" asks Player. "That's why I continue to play."

Player has been helping others most of his professional life. He has been involved in programs for youth for years and is now designing and building golf courses around the world. Player says he has stayed in this aspect of the sport for very specific reasons that fit with his passion and his desire to influence others.

"First of all, I love the game of golf; and secondly, my main business is building golf courses, which I enjoy doing," Player says, "because when you build a good golf course, you're leaving behind something that millions of people are going to play and enjoy; you're leaving something behind."

For Player it is all just a part of making the most of what one has been given, a philosophy he has lived by his entire life.

"I think the most important thing in your life is what sort of a life you lead here on earth. Your faith has got to be the most important thing because that's where you get all your guidance from and all your strength. Now there's nothing wrong in trying to be a winner at whatever you do in life because God likes to see a man who tries, a man who doesn't gives up. You don't have to make a lot of money to be successful. But God hates a coward, and he hates to see a man just being a loafer. He likes to see you work. That's the way I look at it."

The Heart of a Champion is one that understands God's gifts are to be used to impact others:

Certainly Gary Player's accomplishments pushed him to achieve even more in his profession, but more than that, his success inspired him to give. He has spent his entire life in golf finding ways to make the world a better place.

It would be easy for anyone in Gary Player's situation to focus attention on his own needs and desires. Yet this is contrary to the teaching of scripture. We are taught that the more we have, the more we will be expected to give—give of ourselves, give of our time, give of our knowledge, give of our resources. The world can become a better place only when we, in the spirit of Christ, give. God gave us his best when he gave us Jesus, on the cross, as a sacrificial payment for our sin. How much did it cost Him? *Everything.* God gave it all—for us and to us. How then can we not give out of all that we have back to Him by giving to others?

> *"From everyone who has been given*
> *much, much will be demanded; and*
> *from the one who has been entrusted*
> *with much, much more will be asked."*
>
> —Luke 12:48

PERSPECTIVE:

A champion finds God's grace for all situations.

Gary Player is known as one of the kindest and friendliest men to play on the PGA Tour. That the diminutive South African has such a heart of compassion is extraordinary considering the heartache he experienced as a child.

"I lost my mother when I was eight years of age from cancer," Player recalls. "My father was working in the gold mines in South Africa, 14,000 feet underground. My brother was fighting in the last world war alongside the Americans. I was alone most of the time in my youth."

Rather than become bitter over what he had lost, Player is keenly aware of how much he has been blessed.

"It's very difficult when a young boy loses his mother at that age," Player says. "But then you know you look around and you see some children who don't have any parents. So you know, there's always somebody worse off than you are. You know, what God takes away from you, He gives back to you in many, many ways.

"Every day when I go out to work and I see my trophy cabinet and I see 150 championships from all over the world, you realize that it's a talent that is being loaned to you. It's not permanent. It can be taken away from you. So you've got to be very, very thankful."

Player's experience with tragedy has not only given him perspective on his own life, but has also inspired him to use his personal pain as motivation to reach out to others in need.

"It just really makes me very sad when I think of so many children that are left alone," Player said.

Through an outreach located on his property back home, Player is having a daily impact on the lives of South African youth.

"We have this magnificent school on my farm in South Africa for 400 students," says Player. "We feed them twice a day. I'm having people come along and help me—whether it's pencils, or footballs, or books, or any kind of assistance—people have been very kind. The joy that it's given me, it's like winning the Master's tournament, seeing the joy on their faces."

Much of what Player lives out today was imbedded in him through his late mother.

"I always remember her kneeling down and me saying a prayer next to her," Player said reflecting back on his mother's example. "That left a very strong image in my mind."

He has lived by that perspective ever since.

"My Lord is the most important thing in my life, more important than my family," he says. "We've got Somebody to take stock with, Who will help you in trouble, Whom you can rely on, and will give you strength and help you live a decent life. I mean that's the big strength in life."

The Heart of a Champion is one that seeks God's grace in everything:

Gary Player's childhood experience was tragic and painful. Yet instead of becoming bitter, he became better. Player didn't turn inward to shield his pain. Instead, he turned his pain outward to use it as a springboard to help other young people have a better life.

This couldn't have happened had not Player, like his mother, turned to God. In seeking God, Player found hope. He turned his broken past into a fertile ground of growth for others.

It is okay to hurt, and it is okay to express that hurt. Everyone experiences pain in life; no one is immune. What makes a difference in how we find healing and restoration from that hurt is where we go to find it. The love of God is perfect and unconditional, available to us at all times. When we seek it and find it, God's unconditional love gives meaning and purpose to our lives and provides true security. In that love, hurt is healed, our hearts and souls are restored. We can then pass on to others the love, comfort, peace, and hope we have received.

Cast all your anxiety on him because he
cares for you. And the God of all grace,
who called you to his eternal glory in Christ,
after you have suffered a little while,
will himself restore you and make
you strong, firm and steadfast.

—1 Peter 5:7,10

Profiles of **LOREN ROBERTS**

"As a result of my faith growing over the years, I think finally I was able to understand and be in the Lord's will when I was praying out there."

PATIENCE:

A champion is willing to wait for results.

The story of Loren Roberts' career is about learning to wait. Roberts turned pro in 1975 at the age of twenty. But it took six years of trying before he made it to the Tour in 1981. For the next twelve plus years, Roberts searched for his first tournament win. Over a span of nearly 350 tournaments, Roberts steadily climbed the PGA ladder from the 189th-ranked player to 24th. His earnings went from $7,000 to $478,000. Then, in 1994, nearly twenty years after Loren turned pro, he gained his first victory at the Nestle Invitational.

"I like to look at it that I had 12 years to prepare for how I was gonna act," says Roberts of that first win.

The experience was so enjoyable for Roberts that he decided to repeat the feat the following year, winning the Nestle again in 1995. Since then, he has become one of the Tour's upper-echelon players.

"I'm right where I want to be," Roberts says. "I mean, I haven't really suffered a downer. I've really tried to prepare myself with the fact of putting the [first] win behind me. I relish the fact, but I've also been trying to downplay it a little bit."

Waiting is not unusual for Roberts.

"I didn't start playing golf until I was 17 years old," Roberts said. "I studied to be a forest ranger in college; but you don't want to be in the forest when you can be on the golf course, so I became the assistant pro at the country club just for the heck of it."

That's when things started to take shape for Roberts. A retired golf pro moved into the area and began to play at the club where he worked. A few tips and several years later, Roberts was ready for the Tour.

"He said, 'I've noticed a couple of things about you that tell me you have some talent. If you're going to be in the golf business, you should try to play first because if you never do, you'll always regret it if you never gave it a shot,'" said Roberts.

"I think my faith is what's really helped me deal with the fact of being out here for this long without having to win," he says. "I mean, it would have been very easy for me to just walk away and say, 'Well, okay, you know, I can't win out here.'"

The Heart of a Champion is one that is willing to take the long road to reaching goals:

Once Loren Roberts saw his potential, he was willing to put in the necessary work and time to prepare himself to succeed. And he was patient. Roberts knew success would not come overnight; there were way too many areas in which to improve for results to come quickly. So he did not become anxious, but instead he waited for his time to come. Through twelve years, he persevered—practicing and improving; working and waiting—until his day of validation finally came. For Roberts, the "payoff" was worth the wait.

The seed of destiny resides in us all, yet just as a seed needs nutrient-rich soil, water, and sunlight to grow, our seed needs nurturing, encouragement, instruction, and work to mature. That takes time. Unfortunately, we live in a "microwave" culture, where we don't want to wait for anything. The downside of this thinking is that once you quit the first time, it is much easier to quit the next. Quitting impedes growth, and at times even reverses it. So, be patient and remain steadfast, and wait for God's timing to be revealed.

> *Let us not become weary in doing good,*
> *for at the proper time we will reap*
> *a harvest if we do not give up.*
>
> —Galatians 6:9

PERSEVERANCE:

A champion presses on.

P GA Tour veteran Loren Roberts is known as one of the finest putters golf has ever seen. In 1985, just his fifth year on the tour, Roberts was given the nickname "Boss of the Moss" by fellow Tour member David Ogrin, who marveled at his friend's prowess on the greens.

Roberts says it is his faith that enables him to be focused and calm enough to overcome any nerves when it comes to hitting golf's most important strokes.

"I'm always trying to talk to the Lord," Roberts says. "I want the peace of Jesus Christ out there with me on the golf course. As a result of my faith growing over the years, I think finally I was able to understand and be in the Lord's will when I was praying out there. I pray to the Lord and I say, 'Well, Lord, I really want to make this putt, you know. But, Lord, I just want to do the best I can. I want to make this putt, but just help me to understand that whatever happens it's Your will. It's Your plan, and I'll just try to do the best I can. Help me to accept whatever happens."

Roberts is accustomed to rolling in thirty-foot birdie putts at a given tournament. But how about a hole-in-one? Not quite the shot most would expect from the deft putter. When it happened, it surprised nearly everyone on Tour, including Roberts himself.

"A hole in one really is a miracle," Roberts said.

Roberts remembers his ace came in the midst of his playing an unexceptional round of golf. He had struggled a bit just to stay close to the pack. But then, when he least expected it, he made the shot of a lifetime.

"It's kind of funny because . . . I didn't just do anything spectacular," he recalled. "I mean I drove the ball in the fairway; I hit the ball on the green, you know, 15, 20 feet from the hole all day. I didn't make any putts, really. Then I make the bogie at 15 after a poor tee shot. And then I got on the [16th] tee and said, 'Well, you've just been out here treading water all day. Maybe you can make a birdie or two coming in.' And boom! I knocked the thing right in the hole."

The Heart of a Champion is one that keeps pressing on toward the surprises God brings:

While Loren Roberts is a focused and determined player who has worked hard at his craft, he himself was surprised when he made his first ace. The fact that the shot came in the midst of a round that Roberts had struggled through made the happening even sweeter for him. It was a testament to his resiliency and his commitment to press on while performing at a less than desired level. Because he kept a positive outlook and stayed with his game, Roberts received a pleasant surprise.

Golf is all about persevering when the ball is not going in the cup and continuing to look for the next opportunity to make a great shot. In life, when we are laboring and it seems as though we are not making any progress, we must keep going, keep pressing onward, looking for the next opportunity to put the ball in the cup. We never know it, but the hole-in-one may be waiting just around the bend from the hole where we just made bogey. Likewise, in life some great surprise is usually waiting for us after we have pressed through disappointment. Perhaps you are just one hole away—one day, one hour, one dollar, one phone call, one meeting, one prayer. Press on; the surprise of God is closer than you think!

*Let us run with perseverance the race marked
out for us. Let us fix our eyes on Jesus,
the author and perfector of our faith.*

—Hebrews 12:1-2

Profile of JUAN "CHI CHI" RODRIGUEZ

"Life is like golf. If you keep it in the fairway, then you never have to ask for a ruling."

COMPASSION:

A champion has a heart for children.

I t is a common sight: a large group of children gathering after a PGA Senior Tour tournament patiently waiting for their hero to come off the course. Wait, Senior Tour? Hero? Kids? It doesn't compute, unless that Senior golfer is Señor Juan "Chi Chi" Rodriguez.

"The kids come first," Rodriguez told a grown-up autograph seeker who pushed a cap in front of him. "That's what the Bible says."

It's a rule more important to Rodriguez than those of the game. "Why do I love kids?" Rodriguez asked. "Because I was never a kid myself. I was too poor to be a child."

After a tournament round in Arizona, Rodriguez made it a special day for the kids. He was told the group was waiting to see him at the practice tee. So while Jack Nicklaus whacked range balls ten yards away, Rodriguez sat and talked to the kids. He offered words of encouragement or put an arm around each as he signed hats, balls, and programs. Then he quietly gave the group organizer a $100 bill to buy them dinner.

But this was not an unusual scene for Rodriguez. His Chi Chi Rodriguez Foundation in south Florida raises about $800,000 annually for underprivileged children. A school he started through the foundation gives the kids a chance to receive a solid education and a firm grounding in values.

"He probably weighs 145 pounds soaking wet. I don't know how he carries his heart around," says Lee Trevino of his longtime peer. "I don't know anybody who does what he does for kids and charities."

Rodriguez uses golf as a tool to reach children and teach them, and the basis for his philosophy is simple. "Life is like golf," he said. "If you keep it in the fairway, then you never have to ask for a ruling."

The Heart of a Champion is one that has a desire to reach out to youth:

Chi Chi Rodriguez has long been known to golf fans as the sport's ultimate showman. But his peers know him as the ultimate defender of children. Rodriguez invests in the lives of children because he sees them as the future. With fans of all ages clamoring for his attention, Chi Chi devotes his time to kids, even though kids don't help him become any richer financially. Still, Rodriguez knows that his time spent building the lives of kids makes him much richer in ways beyond his wallet.

Through His words, Jesus very clearly emphasizes the importance of children and how they are to be cherished. Jesus freely gave His love to the children, unconditionally. Do you do as Jesus did and bring them into your arms, put your hands on them, and bless them? When we do this, we are Christ-like, living out the principles of the Kingdom of God.

People were bringing little children to Jesus to have him touch them, but the disciples rebuked them. When Jesus saw this, he was indignant. He said to them, "Let the little children come to me, and do not hinder them, for the kingdom of God

belongs to such as these. I tell you the truth, anyone who will not receive the kingdom of God like a little child will never enter it."
And he took the children in his arms, put his hands on them and blessed them.

—Mark 10:13-16

Profiles of SCOTT SIMPSON

"Over three years of asking every question I could think of and reading a whole bunch of books, I became convinced that it was true. That Jesus is who He claimed to be. . . . "

EXCELLENCE:

Champions give their all in every situation.

Each week, as the bustle of life on the PGA Tour unfolds around him—players huddling with agents, meeting and greeting sponsors, and signing autographs for clamoring fans—Scott Simpson seems relaxed and oblivious to it all. He's more interested in posting the week's Bible study schedule.

Simpson's behavior used to be the reason America loved the gentleman's game— sportsmanship. When Simpson won the U.S., Tom Watson shook his hand on the eighteenth green and told him, "Jack Nicklaus once said to me that the best player won here today. Now, I'm saying that to you." That remark still gives Simpson goose bumps.

Simpson stands out in contrast to today's self-centered athletes. He is a champion (1987 U. S. Open) who believes in waiting his turn. In the tradition of Byron Nelson, Simpson is a walking billboard for character and sportsmanship.

That's because as Nelson once was, Simpson now is golf's finest quiet man. While winning a number of tournaments, he has remained almost invisible. Still, it's hard to find anybody who plays the game with more dignity and grace.

Among his peers, Simpson's work habits are almost legendary— undoubtedly the main reason he frequently has been in the hunt for the lead on Sundays. Yet Simpson has been virtually ignored by the surrounding media.

Simpson is too plain for today's journalists. He is a devoted family man who is only seen with his wife and children. He's a devout Christian intellectual who lives his principles instead of advertising them. He works hard, plays clean, and doesn't talk about himself.

His idea of a great way to relieve the tensions of a rough day on the course is to take his kids to a good theme park or waterslide. On the course his attitude is similar—steady. But, it's not that easy to figure Simpson out. He is likely to show up at a contemporary music concert, loves the NBA, and has a sense of humor. He married his high school sweetheart—"She asked me out because I was too shy," he says—and honeymooned at the Walker Cup to save money. All the while he was trying to decide whether he would become a stockbroker or a teacher.

"On the course, Scott is so good he's almost—I hate to say it— boring," says his friend Larry Mize. "He's down the middle of the fairway and almost always putting for birdie. Nothing seems to rattle him one way or another. You play a round with him, and you don't seem to notice what he's doing. But later it hits you how awesome he was."

The Heart of a Champion is devoted to excellence in every area:

Whether it is his family, his friendships, his faith, or his approach to his profession, Scott Simpson gives all of himself, yet he does so with an ease rather than obsession. If that makes him boring, then more athletes should be so boring.

Do you keep the same standard of excellence for your family as you do your work? Do you keep the same standards for your faith as you do your friends? God's Word tells us we are to do all things with excellence as if we are doing these things as an offering to

Him. We tend to think of excellence in terms of performance at work or church. I'm led to believe that God's standard of excellence for us entails things like returning phone calls promptly, paying bills on time, telling the truth always, and giving undivided attention to your spouse and children. This is excellence. Do you walk in it?

Whatever you do, work at it with all your heart, as working for the Lord, not men, since you know that you will receive an inheritance from the Lord as a reward. It is the Lord Christ you are serving.

—Colossians 3:23-24

FAITH:

A champion seeks truth.

When Scott Simpson began his quest for truth, he started from a place of disbelief. Yet, he earnestly desired to know the truth. So in 1981 he became involved in the PGA Tour Bible study and began to debate deep issues with the Christian players on the tour. Simpson needed to be convinced.

"I didn't believe any of it growing up," says Simpson. "I had looked at Buddhism and the new age kind of the thing—psychology and all that stuff—for basically trying to be a better golfer. I was just curious if any of that was true—any religion—or if there really was a God. It was more curiosity than anything. I approach things pretty intellectually, and couldn't buy into this Christian stuff at all. The only problem was my wife was a Christian. So I wanted to prove her wrong, prove how stupid it was to believe in these old myths and rules."

"So, I went to the discussion group, and we started talking about good and evil. It was with Larry Moody who leads our Bible study. We were talking about hypocrites. Actually, I was telling him, 'You know, I don't like some of these Christians anyway. I don't want to be like these guys.' And he challenged me to find out about Jesus Christ and what was true or false, but don't judge my basis of religion on somebody else—you know, whether it's a great person I admire or it's someone that I don't admire. He told me to learn about Jesus—is it true? What about Buddha? Is it true? Mohammed?

I was challenged to just start finding out if the Bible was true. I'd always just totally rejected it; you know, intellectually it just couldn't be true. . . .

"So, I started reading and doing research with the whole idea of proving it [Jesus] wrong. And over three years of asking every question I could think of and reading a whole bunch of books, I became convinced that it was true. That Jesus is who He claimed to be; that He is God; that He actually was crucified—a historical fact the same way we believe that Lincoln was president— Jesus really was here, He was crucified, and He really did come back from the dead. And proof that there's something beyond this life to look forward to. Through finding out what Jesus really stood for and what He taught, and what it meant to be a follower of Jesus Christ—what it meant to be a Christian—I finally understood that's where the real freedom was. . . .

"The only reason I decided to become a Christian was because it was true. I couldn't argue with it anymore."

The Heart of a Champion is one that seeks after truth:

Scott Simpson had been exposed to all kinds of philosophies, had examined them, and realized absolute truth could not be found in any of them. But what Simpson did then was atypical. Rather than making conclusions based on feelings or past experiences, he sought truth through research to prove or disprove the Christian faith. What he found was irrefutable, historical evidence that proved the truth of Christ and His deity. Because he sought truth, Simpson found truth.

No matter where you are in your faith journey, do you aggressively pursue truth? We are told in Scripture that those who seek will find, those who knock shall have the door opened for them. We are encouraged to keep knocking until we find answers. A recent survey has revealed that over 75 percent of the American public make key life decisions based on their feelings and reject the idea of absolute truth. Do you continue to seek truth in God's word, or do you make decisions based on feelings or your own religious tradition? Keep seeking. Keep knocking. God holds all truth and will make known to you the truths you need to find.

*"You will seek me and find me when
you seek me with all your heart."*

—Jeremiah 29:13

PEACE:

A champion is not ruffled by circumstances.

At the 1987 U.S. Open, Scott Simpson held off Tom Watson down the stretch of the tournament's final round and beat Watson by one shot in a victory most experts predicted would not happen. Golf pundits figured the seemingly unemotional Simpson would wilt under final-round pressure with one of the sport's greatest champions breathing down his neck. But Simpson stunned them all.

"That was a big thrill, the U. S. Open; something I'd dreamed about since I was a kid," Simpson recalls.

"It just so happened that the week before, I was trying real hard and pressing—trying to get ready for the U. S. Open—and was getting real frustrated because I didn't play very well," Simpson remembers. "That week I put a scripture in my pocket, which I don't normally do, but I was working on just being content and not getting so frustrated. It was Colossians 3:17, 'Whatever you do, in word or deed, do it all in the name of the Lord Jesus, giving thanks through him to God, the Father.'"

The refocusing eased the pressure for Simpson.

"I just played all that week just kind of thankful; just thankful to be there," Simpson says. "It seemed to take a lot of the pressure off for me. So, at even the last nine holes, I wasn't trying to worry too much about Tom Watson, but just trying to play my own game. I was just real fortunate that it worked out that way.

"Without that freedom I think there's just so much more pressure on you," Simpson states emphatically. "I know when I won the Open, I talked about that afterwards with the press, because they were asking me, 'You've got Tom Watson breathing down your back, and you've never won a Major before.' And yet I was smiling. I was having a great time, knowing that I really wanted to win, but if I didn't win, hey, you know second isn't bad; you know, I'm doing the best I can.

"That was my goal that week was to do the best I could. And, you know, Colossians 3:17, I was just going to do whatever I could, in His name, just to be the best I could. So I went out there and was having a good time and was fortunate enough to win. Then I went in there and shared that in the pressroom. . . .

"I know before I was a Christian everything was performance based. If I played great, I felt great. I felt like I was really somebody and doing what I was supposed to do. But if I played bad, had a bad streak, I mean I felt terrible; I felt like, *What a loser!* Now if I play poorly, I know I'm not playing well, but I know I am not a loser. So, there's a subtle but really important difference there."

The Heart of a Champion is one that keeps God's peace even under pressure:

In releasing the pressure to God, Scott Simpson received a sense of freedom that allowed him to play golf's biggest tournament like he was in the midst of a practice round on his home course. The result was one of golf's greatest surprise champions.

When you are under pressure, are you constantly trying to figure out how you can fix the situation? God never promised there would not be stress around us, but He did promise that He would be with us in the stress. Once Jesus was in a boat with His disciples when a massive storm arose. While the disciples feared, Jesus rose and calmed the storm. Sometimes He will calm the storms in our lives. At other times He will calm us in the midst of the storm. Either way, we have access to His peace. In the storms of life, listen for His voice. Receive His peace and be freed from the pressures those storms can bring.

Do not be anxious about anything, but in everything, by prayer and petition, with thanksgiving, present your requests to God. And the peace of God, which transcends all understanding, will guard your hearts and your minds in Christ Jesus.

—Philippians 4:6-7

PERSPECTIVE:

A champion sees God's hand in all things.

Since joining the PGA Tour in 1978, Scott Simpson has enjoyed more than ten tournament championships both in the U.S. and abroad; top-ten finishes in all four of golf's major championships; and over six million dollars in career earnings. The disappointments have been few.

But in 1999, Simpson experienced adversity when he suffered a broken ankle in a skiing accident. The injury forced him to miss the entire 2000 season and, later, to play with a noticeable limp, all of which created significant challenges to making it back.

"It was real good skiing," Simpson says with a big grin. "It wasn't that bad a break. It was just right above the ankle and because it wasn't bad, my doctor said, 'Well, it's borderline. You don't need to have surgery . . . probably.' So we just put it in a boot, and it was supposed to heal up."

What resulted was a frustrating sequence of events that Simpson endured for over a year.

"After six months of waiting for the bones to heal, I had to go in for surgery and then two-and-a-half months on crutches. So, I ended up missing a whole year."

What started as a bad break turned out to be a blessing.

"With my kids being teenagers, it was a great year to be home," said Simpson. "So, I think in some ways it was a blessing, really. I had talked to my wife about, you know, after 20 years thinking, *Gosh, I'd love a sabbatical for a while.* I was just tired of the traveling more than anything and doing the same thing day after day—practicing and playing.

"I always had a two-week rule where I would only be gone for two weeks, and either I would go home or they would come out on tour. And we pretty much kept to that through the kids growing up. . . . The great thing is, God gave me a break—literally! It was a great time to be home."

The time at home also revitalized his passion for the game of golf.

"In a lot of ways it's really fired me up," Simpson said, "and I found myself saying, 'Gosh, I really do love to play.' You know, anytime something like that's taken away from you, you have to evaluate it. I said, 'Wow! You know, I really did like that.' So, I've been working harder and I'm going to give it a great try. It refreshed my enthusiasm for the game."

The Heart of a Champion is one that understands God has a purpose in everything:

When Scott Simpson's leg did not heal properly his frustration could have turned to anger. Instead, Simpson spent quality time with his wife and children for an entire year, a luxury he had before not been able to afford. Then, when the time off provided for a restoration of Simpson's passion for his golf career, Simpson realized that he had been doubly blessed.

So often when something hits us that is difficult or inconvenient, we turn and ask God, "Why me?" At times we think He is working against us. At times we think He isn't working at all. Why? Go ahead and be blunt with yourself: A part of us deep down feels that we really know a better way than God does. The real problem is that we don't completely trust God. Yet He tells us His ways are perfect and that He is constantly turning what was meant for evil into something good. Over thousands of years, God has never let His children down. What makes us think He is about to become flawed, too busy, or uncaring now?

It is God who works in you to will and
to act according to his good purpose.

—Philippians 2:13

"I've got to come back quicker than the average guy. And the faster I come back and forget about it, the better off I am."

SELF-CONTROL:

Champions keep their emotions in check.

G olf can be a tremendously frustrating sport. Timing in the swing can mean the difference between putting the ball three feet from the cup or in the lake. One missed shot can cost a player thousands of dollars. Composure is paramount, and losing emotional control can bring disastrous results.

Paul Stankowski remembers a tournament in 2000 where his emotions were tested:

"I was nine under for the day with two holes to play on Sunday. I hit a seven iron into the 17th hole. The pin is on the left side of the green. I was aggressive. I took it right of the pin. I pulled it a little bit. It bounced and it went into the water. I wasn't too mad at that. I made an aggressive play and hit the blue line average shot that went into the water. Now I could have blocked it 40 yards right in the bunker and got up and down and made par. But I'd have been a chicken. I'd have felt like I'd bailed out. I was aggressive. I saw my target, I fired at it, I didn't pull it off. But that was okay; I can handle that."

"It's when I'm scared, and I hold on to it and I hit it right into the bunker, and now I'm playing the bunker, and from there I hit my bunker shot bad; and I three-putt and make it—that would frustrate me. I'd rather make a double [bogey] by hitting an aggressive shot, than make a double [bogey] by being scared. So, it's a total mental approach. What, what are you focused on? If I'm focused on the right things; and I make an aggressive swing, confident swing, and it doesn't work out, well, that's a physical mistake—things happen.

"Execution is the key. You need to execute your shot; think about execution. The result? Sometimes you can't control results out here. You hit a shot and a gust of wind comes up and it blows your ball in the water. You can't control it. Are you mad at yourself? No. Physical errors happen, and I can deal with that. A mental mistake, I can't take it. That's where I've got to come back quicker than the average guy. And the faster I come back and forget about it, the better off I am."

The Heart of a Champion is one that stays cool under pressure:

Think about the intensity of a major golf tournament, the press, and the pressure. Just one mistake can mean Paul Stankowski walks away with thousands of dollars less than he would have. Stankowski has little tolerance for mental errors. Why? Because he feels he should be able to guard himself against them. Self-control is not only being able to turn away from a bad situation once we've encountered it, but also doing what is necessary to make sure we don't get into that situation in the first place.

In the same way people recovering from alcohol addiction don't wander into a liquor store to read the labels, we must be careful about putting ourselves in situations where our emotions can get the better of us. Emotional self-control can be the same as exercising wisdom. Often when we become emotional over an issue, we respond out of that emotion and do not exercise wisdom. Words that are spoken in the heat of passion or emotion can be binding and create great difficulties for us. Actions that come out of a similar time can bring about irreversible consequences. To be self-controlled emotionally means not letting emotions overcome rational thought and wisdom. Emotion without self-control has led to abuses of power, regrettable decisions, and the destruction of that which is precious. Emotion under self-control has led to great human achievement—the building of great cultures, societal changes, racial equality, and the relief of human suffering. Emotion is good and necessary, but without self-control it can be dangerous.

> *Better a patient man than a warrior,*
> *a man who controls his temper*
> *than one who takes a city.*
>
> —Proverbs 16:32

PERSPECTIVE:

A champion knows the source for direction.

The line between hitting the ball without analyzing the process and scrutinizing every element of the swing is fine. Paul Stankowski has been on both sides of that line in his quest for greater consistency. Still, he knows it is possible to analyze too much and end up with mental overload.

"If I'm struggling with my golf swing—not hitting the ball well, not knowing where it's going to go—I'll start thinking about it," says Stankowski. "And you start tinkering and all of a sudden you're going to get worse. And then you're in the hole. Where usually your first thought is the best thought.

"I just find my yardage because 158 yards, that's a solid eight iron—period—if there's no wind and we're at sea level. So, there's no thinking that's involved. If the pin is on the right side of the green, I like to cut the ball, start at 15 feet left of the hole, and I'll hit my eight iron 158 yards. I mean it's a simple game. So there's really no reason to over-think. I just take it down the line and hit it. There's no thought. But when I start thinking, usually the thoughts are not where I want to hit the ball. That isn't fine."

Thinking is certainly a large part of the game, but it is what Stankowski allows his mind to dwell on that makes all the difference.

"You can think about where you want to hit it, how high you want to hit it, what kind of shot you want to hit. That's fine," Stankowski says. "Overload comes when you start thinking about your swing: Where do you want to be on your backswing? What kind of position do I need to be in? Where am I on the leader board? Where am I on the money list? Who's watching? What time is my flight home tomorrow night? That type of thing. That's stuff you don't need to be thinking about. Those are distractions. So you can think all you want about how far you are, what kind of wind is blowing—there are a lot of things you need to think about, and take those into consideration. But it's separating the distractions from the facts [that is important]. And the fact is you need to hit a good golf shot. The distractions you don't need."

To help with his mental approach, Stankowski frequently refers back to the yardage book. The yard book tells him everything he needs to know about each hole on the course he is playing—distance, hazards, normal wind direction, and other aspects he will need to know to navigate the course. To Stankowski, the yard book is a help in more than one way.

"The yard book for me means two things: one, it's information; two, it kind of gets me in my routine. So when the hole is over and I write the score down, I put that scorecard underneath the page. I flip it [the page] and now I'm on the next hole. I look and see how far it is to the next bunker. So now I'm focused on the next hole instead of what's behind me. And that's a good way to get yourself out of whatever just happened and focus on the next shot. And that's huge."

The Heart of a Champion is one that looks to God's Word for guidance:

Paul Stankowski still has moments when he can over-analyze his game. When that happens, he can think himself into a real mess. So, when he is over-thinking or facing adverse situations, Stankowski turns to his yardage book to become more focused, to forget what has just happened, and to press on to the next hole, the next shot. The yardage book gives Stankowski renewed vision and direction for his game.

God's Word is intended to be our daily "yardage book." You need direction for whatever comes next. You also need something to take your mind off of what just happened and get you focused on what is ahead. The Word of God will do that and more. God's Word illuminates our way, gives us wisdom for critical decision-making, and gets us focused on what lies ahead of us, rather than what lies behind. Do you view every decision through the lens of scripture? If not, you should begin now. You will gain wisdom, direction, focus, and perspective.

> ***Your word is a lamp to my feet***
> ***and a light for my path.***
>
> —Psalm 119:105

"The peace I have now is so wonderful. I don't understand how I lived so long without it. I'm proud of the fact that my faith in God is so much stronger, and I'm so much more at peace with myself than I've ever been in my life."

FAITH:

A champion's true character is easily recognized by others.

f ever a golfer seemed born to win a major, it was Payne Stewart. With a vibrant personality and classic swing, he had the elements of a star. His personality was engaging and incomparable. His swing was flat-out beautiful. The combination of affability and ability made Stewart one of the Tour's most popular players. Yet at times Stewart's life seemed enigmatic, as well, as if he was searching for something.

"He was asking these life and God questions for several years," says Bobby Clampett. "He was asking: 'What is my purpose in life? How did I get here? Who made this world? What's our reason for living?' Lots of important questions."

Somewhere in his quest, Stewart found what was missing. The result was undeniable. Fans recognized it; so did the media and Payne's peers.

"Payne had definitely turned his life around," said Scott Simpson. "He'd always been a fun guy. But he was kind of cocky and didn't always care about other people. Before he died though, he had really changed as a person. And everyone noticed it. He cared a lot about people. He was just a different person."

"We started to see something new, something totally different," said friend and fellow pro, Paul Azinger. "We saw a man who was as interested in people as he was in golf, a man who played to win but truly loved others at the same time. Payne became gracious in victory and gracious in defeat. Only God could do that, because only God changes hearts. Everyone who knew Payne saw this dramatic change in his life."

"I mean *everybody* noticed a change in his life," says Larry Mize. "Not that he was a bad guy before, but that Jesus really shined through him the last couple of years of his life. It was just phenomenal."

"Did I see a different person? Or did I just see his good parts?" asks Lee Janzen rhetorically. "Maybe we just saw his good parts more often. I think he was always capable of being like that.

"And I guess that's the biggest testimony there, that you could see the difference instead of him having to tell us the difference. So he could tell us why."

At the 1999 U. S. Open, Stewart told the world why. This, it seemed, was the moment he had been born for. In draining a fifteen-foot putt on the final hole, Stewart captured his second Open title and third win in a major. In victory, he embraced runner-up Phil Mickelson, then raised an arm clad with a *What-Would-Jesus-Do* bracelet and gave thanks to God. At once, everyone knew something was different about Payne.

Early in the '99 season, Stewart's ten-year-old son, Aaron, had given his dad the bracelet and challenged him to let others know about his commitment to Christ. It was like telling a Sphinx to keep silent. Payne let the world know.

"There used to be a void in my life," Payne told the press shortly after the dramatic win. "The peace I have now is so wonderful. I don't understand how I lived so long without it. I'm proud of the fact that my faith in God is so much stronger, and I'm so much more at peace with myself than I've ever been in my life."

The Heart of a Champion is one that demonstrates the character of God:

When Payne Stewart's life changed, the evidence of the power of God in his life was undeniable for others. They recognized the reason by the way Payne reflected Christ. While Payne was not a bad person early on in life, he seemed to be a man who was missing something. Friends described him as missing peace or maturity or confidence or security. In whichever way it showed up, the fact remains that once Payne committed his life to God, that void was no longer apparent. It wasn't about bumper stickers, bracelets, or T-shirts that advertised his faith. It was about something real and different that others saw in him. This was the life of Christ manifest in Payne.

Have you ever wondered how people around you know what you believe? Is it because you have bumper stickers and posters that express your beliefs? Is it because you are always talking about what you believe or because you have membership with a certain club or faith organization? *Or is it because you live what you believe?* When we live our lives based on our conviction, it shows. Does your life demonstrate the life of Christ in you? Or does it merely demonstrate that you know all about Christ? There is a difference. The Bible tells us that the world will know followers of Christ by the "fruit" that is manifest in their lives. So, how does your fruit look?

"I am the vine; you are the branches.
If a man remains in me and I in him,
he will bear much fruit; apart from me
you can do nothing. This is to my
Father's glory, that you bear much fruit,
showing yourselves to be my disciples."

—John 15:5,8

INFLUENCE:

A champion influences others.

The tragic plane crash that claimed Payne Stewart's life in November of 1999 came just five months after his dramatic win at the 1999 U. S. Open. A stunned golf community was left to reflect on the life of a man who touched them all.

"It was a tragedy, Payne going home early," said Larry Mize. "You know, as much as I know where he is, it's still very difficult to know that he's gone."

"I think Payne was in a place where he wasn't afraid of dying because he knew there was something better," says Scott Simpson.

As difficult as it was for his peers to handle Payne Stewart's sudden death, one thing became quickly clear—the tragic loss had a sobering effect on many of them. It caused some to reevaluate their own lives and make significant changes.

"I think Payne's death had a big impact on the tour," said Simpson, "and I think it's rippled across everyone who plays golf. Because here's a guy at the top of his game, top of his life really, and he'd come out and pretty publicly talked about his new faith in Christ—and how much he did turn to God and what a difference that made in his life before he won the U. S. Open. I think it impacted a lot of people that say, "Gosh, you know, maybe there's something to this."

"It got everybody thinking about their own lives I think—about how quickly your life can be snuffed out," said Steve Jones, "and how you really need to think about what's going to happen when you die."

"Guys have had to take stock of their life," concurs Larry Mize, "and say, 'Wait a second. You know what? Payne had it all, and he realized that it's all about Jesus. It's not about me, or what I do on the golf course, or anything like that. It's about what Jesus has done for me.'"

Tom Lehman spoke at Stewart's emotional memorial service. "I've got just a zillion letters from people who have talked about how it's changed their lives," he says, "and how they watched his funeral, and they listened to people talking, and how because of that they realized that they were missing something. It really goes back to the fact that when you're faced with that kind of a tragedy, it makes you realize your own mortality; and it makes you realize the need that you do have for God."

Perhaps no player on the PGA tour was affected by Stewart's death as much as good friend Lee Janzen, who was moved to make life-altering decisions.

"Payne Stewart's death probably has had a more profound affect in my life than any other thing that I can think of," says Janzen. "Just to think of how tomorrow is guaranteed to no one. And it's so important to have your life as much as possible in order. You know, the people that you love, they need to know that. And you need to show them. You can't just tell them. You have to show them."

The Heart of a Champion is one that is prepared to impact the lives of others:

It is rare that a man has the opportunity to have a profound and life-changing affect on others. In Payne Stewart's case, this came about through tragedy. The tragic events of Payne's death caused his peers and friends to reevaluate their lives and what they had considered to be truly important. Death has a way of doing that to us. We pause and take stock of our own lives. We ask ourselves if we have been living for the right reasons. In the case of Payne Stewart, his death caused many to say, "It could have easily been me. Payne was ready to go. Would I have been ready?" The self-introspection brought about by Payne's death led many of Payne's peers to follow the lead of their friend and put their trust in Christ.

Are you a person of impact? How do you know? According to the teachings of Jesus, a person of impact is one whom others want to be like. When others come into contact with that person, they see something appealing. They recognize they do not have whatever that is, and they need it and want it. The Son of God was so appealing He was irresistible. Being in His presence made all kinds of people want to follow Him, speak intimately with Him, sit at His feet, and be like Him. They wanted what He had on the inside. We don't have to be concerned with doing and saying the "right" things, wearing the "right" clothes, or having the "right" Christian phrases. All we need to do is let Christ live through us. It is not about doing. It is about being. So just be what He has called you to become and let Him live and love through you. In you, He will be irresistible to others.

> *"You are the light of the world. A city on a hill cannot be hidden. Neither do people light a lamp and put it under a bowl. Instead they put it on its stand, and it gives light to everyone in the house. In the same way, let your light shine before men, that they may see your good deeds and praise your Father in heaven."*
>
> —Matthew 5:14-16

About the Author

Steve Riach is president and cofounder of VisionQuest Communications Group, Inc., a Dallas-based media company. Along with being a popular author and speaker, he is an award-winning producer, writer, and director of television and film projects and is one of the nation's foremost creators of virtuous sports content. He is also cofounder of the Heart of a Champion Foundation, a non-profit organization that has created an innovative program to teach character and virtue in schools. Steve and his family reside in Colleyville, Texas.

Heart of a Champion

Heart of a Champion is a registered trademark under which virtuous sports products and programs are created and distributed. Materials include award-winning videos, television and radio programs, films, books, and Internet activities. To learn more about Heart of a Champion resources, products, or programming, call 972-690-4588, or visit the Web site at www.heartofachampion.org.

The Heart of a Champion Foundation is an independent, national nonprofit organization utilizing the platform of sports to build and reinforce character and virtue in young people. Blending the message and the messenger, the Heart of a Champion Foundation's winning formula teaches and models character education at the grassroots level, to mold better citizens and develop the heart of a champion in youth.

The Heart of a Champion school program is a unique, in-class character education program that teaches positive character values and traits through video, audio, and written vignettes featuring popular and respected athletes and other individuals. Teaching virtues through "sight and sound" stories of positive role models attracts the attention of learners and arouses their interest, raising questions that lead to discussions and reflections about the implementation of those virtues into the daily life process. Stories that demonstrate values such as honesty, perseverance, courage, commitment, discipline, integrity, and fairness, encourage students to recognize and follow their examples. The Heart of a Champion program also includes student, teacher, and parent enrichment materials to reinforce the positive character traits that are taught and discussed. The Heart of a Champion Foundation believes that teaching kids character and virtue can help build the champions of tomorrow through stories of the heroes of today. For more information, visit the Web site at www.heartofachampion.org, or call (972) 497-8538.

Additional copies of this book are available
from your local bookstore.

Other devotional and gift book titles:

Passion for the Game
Above the Rim
The Drive to Win
Inspire a Dream
It's How You Play the Game
Life Lessons from Auto Racing

If you have enjoyed this book,
or if it has impacted your life,
we would like to hear from you.

Please contact us at:

Honor Books
An Imprint of Cook Communication Ministries
4050 Lee Vance View
Colorado Springs, CO 89018

www.cookministries.com